D1415612

Getting Beyond
Bullying and
Exclusion
PreK–5

Getting Beyond
Bullying and
Exclusion
PreK–5

Empowering Children in
Inclusive Classrooms

Ronald Mah

Skyhorse Publishing

DISCARDED

LIBRARY
CALDWELL COMMUNITY COLLEGE
HUDSON, NC

Copyright © 2009 by Corwin
First Skyhorse Publishing edition 2013

12-13 BT11.44

All Rights Reserved. No part of this book may be reproduced in any manner
without the express written consent of the publisher, except in the case of brief
excerpts in critical reviews or articles. All inquiries should be addressed to Skyhorse
Publishing, 307 West 36th Street, 11th Floor, New York, NY 10018.

Skyhorse Publishing books may be purchased in bulk at special discounts for
sales promotion, corporate gifts, fund-raising, or educational purposes. Special
editions can also be created to specifications. For details, contact the Special Sales
Department, Skyhorse Publishing, 307 West 36th Street, 11th Floor, New York, NY
10018 or info@skyhorsepublishing.com.

Skyhorse® and Skyhorse Publishing® are registered trademarks of Skyhorse
Publishing, Inc.®, a Delaware corporation.

www.skyhorsepublishing.com

10 9 8 7 6 5 4 3 2 1

Library of Congress Cataloging-in-Publication Data is available on file.

ISBN: 978-1-62087-878-1

Printed in China

Contents

Acknowledgments

They said the kids hung out in Linda's classroom fifth period. We had just spent the weekend on a retreat organized by the Asian Student Union at Berkeley High School. My friends had been involved with the ASU, but the retreat was my first time participating. It was really cool, hanging out, sharing common interests and concerns. Now it was Monday back at school, and I remembered about hanging out at lunchtime in Linda's classroom. Linda Wing taught history and was the ASU sponsor.

I opened the door. A couple of dozen kids—American-born, foreign-born, mostly Asian but some other kids too—eating lunch, talking, and laughing. Linda was sitting at her desk, in her mid-twenties, barely older than we were. I entered. She turned her face to me. And . . . and she said, "Hi Ronald." My heart leapt! She said, "Hi, Ronald." I was so moved—she knew my name! I'm important enough to remember my name? At a time in my life when I sometimes felt invisible, when I wasn't sure of who or what I was, she saw, knew, and acknowledged me. "Hi, Ronald." That moment and through other experiences, Linda made me feel special and important. I graduated and then worked with her as a teacher's aide, coming down from UC Berkeley almost every day. She helped so many other kids feel important during those years.

This book is dedicated to Linda and the other teachers that touch hearts and inspire the souls of kids. She inspired me to want to be like her. To help children feel important, like she made me—us—feel important. To Linda and the teachers who touch our hearts, thanks for inspiring us to touch children at the times in their lives.

PUBLISHER'S ACKNOWLEDGMENTS

We gratefully acknowledge the following peer reviewers for their editorial insight and guidance:

Karen Thomes, MEd/ECSE
Early Childhood Special Educator
Indian Island School
Indian Island, ME

Kathryn Underwood
Assistant Professor
School of Early Childhood Education
Ryerson University
Toronto, ON, Canada

About the Author

**Ronald Mah**, an educator and licensed marriage and family therapist, has worked in early childhood education for sixteen years. A credentialed elementary and secondary teacher, he is the author of *Difficult Behavior in Early Childhood* and *The One-Minute Temper Tantrum Solution* (2006 and 2008, Corwin). He wrote the Asian Pacific Islander Parent Education Support curriculum (Department of Human Services–San Francisco, 1996). Ronald has been featured in DVDs on child development and behavior (Fixed Earth Films) and has been involved in community and high school mental health clinics, and severe emotional disturbance, at-risk youth, welfare-to-work, and Head Start programs. As a graduate college instructor and board of directors member of the California Association of Marriage and Family Therapists and of the California Kindergarten Association, Ronald combines concepts, principles, and philosophy with practical techniques and guidelines for effective and productive results. Ronald has a psychotherapy practice in San Leandro, California, where he works with children, teens, adults, couples, and families.

Introduction

INCLUSION MEANS . . .

Educational, social, economic, and political policy often collides with classroom reality. The inclusive classroom is a wonderful concept, but also a complex day-to-day challenge for teachers. Problematic behaviors already disrupting classroom communities, specifically exclusion and bullying, may intensify with greater inclusion of child diversity. The reality of modern education means children with a variety of learning and processing abilities and issues are in the general classroom, often with more and different academic and behavior problems. Principles of an inclusive classroom to address the challenges of learning and processing differences are similar to principles addressing socioeconomic diversities of race, ethnicity, religion, class, and family composition. Caring adults hope that children naturally accept each other, interacting with respect, appreciation, and kindness. Everyone wishes that were true, but if wishes simply just came true, then we'd all have ponies! Reality as testified to by veteran teachers' experiences, however, is that it is much more difficult. Children with challenges often experience misunderstanding and mistreatment by classmates, especially those with aggressive tendencies due to their own issues. When teachers are able to create respectful classroom communities, they become a joy in which to learn and teach. Children learn to relate to classmates in healthy and productive relationships predictive of fellow citizens in society.

This book will focus on children with one or more of four specific challenges: children with learning disabilities or differences (LD), children with attention deficit hyperactivity disorder (ADHD), children with Asperger syndrome (AS), and children with gifted abilities. The principles for supporting these children can be both derived from principles supporting all children and applied to children with various other challenges. Children with challenges are often in need of skilled and conceptually sound adult support. Diagnoses or labels represent higher or lower extremes on normal continuums of abilities or challenges. The more teachers become aware of the knowledge, skills, and wisdom acquired working in the typical classroom with a familiar spectrum of child diversity, the more they can apply that to working with and supporting children with specific challenges. Conversely, the more teachers become aware of their knowledge, skills, and wisdom acquired working with children with LD, ADHD, AS, and gifted abilities, the more they can apply that to working with and supporting a diversity of children in typical classrooms.

A functional definition of culture is that it consists of attitudes, values, beliefs, and behaviors that promote survival in a given context. The context of concern is a community with particular environmental requirements and challenges. The cultural adaptations in one context may or may not be cross-culturally effective in a new context. Specifically, moving from a supported environment such as home or a special education class to a general education classroom (or from one classroom to another), with new classmates or a new teacher will be cross-culturally challenging. Areas of survival include academic, social, emotional, psychological, and spiritual functioning. Children with LD, ADHD, AS, or gifted abilities may develop problematic attitudes, values, and beliefs for survival prior to and in the mainstream classroom. This may be expressed in sometimes unfathomable behaviors.

The book will examine the dynamic of adult attention, nurturing, and guidance for all kinds of children while focusing on the four challenges named above. Topics examined for typically developing children and children with the four types of challenges include the following:

- How to build powerful successful children
- Social emotional intelligence
- Resiliency
- Eleven reasons individuals may miss the social cues that facilitate interpersonal relationships
- The dynamics of victims and bullying
  - Specific issues for each of the four groups
- Relational aggression
- The Ninety-Second-a-Day Self-Esteem Prescription Plan

The classroom community exists to meet the academic needs of children. It also functions to facilitate emotional, psychological, and social development, whether or not that is the expressed intent of the teacher, school, or district. I am an educator-turned-psychotherapist who is still involved in education (training, consulting, and writing). I find that individual and group behaviors, emotional and psychological health, and children's individual challenges fundamentally influence academic development. I often assess children with coexisting behavior and academic problems. I usually find significant social-emotional problems along with learning and processing issues. Children with the greatest problems almost always have a complexity of issues. Fortunately, issue by issue, and in combination, children's dynamics and functioning make sense. Thus, teachers and other adults, including parents, can address and support children's needs and foster their strengths while compensating for challenges. Generally, children who are ready to learn and be taught are happy children. And happy children learn more readily. Anything academically empowering or stimulating facilitates children's self-esteem, happiness, and social satisfaction. The diverse classroom must integrate prior academic and social-emotional strengths and weaknesses, successes and failures with current challenges for all its students.

INCLUSION MEANS MORE

More LD, ADHD, AS, and Giftedness

Special education services are often curtailed despite the mandates of the American Disabilities Act. Finding special education teachers is challenging.

> Historically, teachers trained to work with children with special needs have been difficult to find. According to the group Recruiting New Teachers, 98 percent of school districts have reported shortages in special education professionals. A reason cited by several in the field is overall lack of interest from prospective teachers. (Gaetano, 2006, ¶ 5)

With the right to an equitable education, shortages of special education teachers, and more rigid criteria for special education services, the result is that many children with learning issues are now placed in general education classes. There always have been children with undiagnosed challenges in general classrooms (especially *that* kid in your classroom!), but now children with identified diagnoses are often placed into general classrooms without additional or minimal educational support. Greater diversity in many forms may increase percentages of children with academic and behavioral difficulty. Children with different or quirky behaviors have always been a part of classrooms. Teachers who never heard of high functioning autism (hfASD or HFA) or AS find children with these issues in their classrooms more regularly. Or they now have a diagnosis for the odd behaviors they have seen for years.

Children with gifted abilities are in classrooms with needs that challenge teachers. This occurs whether or not there are effective gifted and talented education (GATE) programs in the schools. The mother of a middle-school boy said, "They designated him as gifted long ago. But from early elementary school to now, they haven't taught him any differently from regular education kids." She felt that he had not gotten any benefit from being identified as having gifted abilities. He expressed his gifts anyway (in particular, his creative verbal skills). Subsequently, he developed a reputation of being a nice kid who would not shut up! Other parents have complained it seems like children with gifted abilities are somehow expected to teach themselves. Meeting heightened academic needs, while providing appropriate emotional and social support, intimidates some teachers. This is in addition to dealing with parents aggressively advocating for their children.

> "Some teachers have an attitude of, 'That's not who I signed up to teach, that's not my problem, that's not my kid,' and that's an attitude problem," said Amy Dell, who is the chairwoman of the Special Education Department at The College of New Jersey. (Gaetano, 2006, ¶ 6)

Some overwhelmed teachers want fewer, not more, demands. Fewer challenges, fewer behavior problems, and less diversity translate into easier children, classrooms, teaching, and . . . less requirement to be outstanding teachers! Fortunately, most teachers want to be those great teachers.

INCLUSION MEANS LESS

Less Time and Energy, Fewer Resources, and *More* Responsibility

Children with significant challenges often disproportionately draw teachers' already scarce time and energy. Inclusion of children with special needs may mean overall less time and energy for many teachers to teach. This becomes especially true with current administrative and political demands for educational accountability and academic standards. Despite greater diversity, there are often fewer resources. Resource and specialty teachers may go the way of full-time school nurses, counselors, and assistant principals. Teachers and other educators suffer the greater demands and responsibility without greater resources in other countries as well. For example, from Great Britain, Steve Sinnott, leader of the National Union of Teachers states, "The inclusion of children with special educational needs in mainstream schools is carried out without sufficient preparation and resources" (Pupils "should penalise bullies," 2007, Special needs section, ¶ 3).

EDUCATIONAL CHALLENGE

Educational challenge is intensified with more students with varied aptitudes and challenges. Although federal and state laws mandate mainstreaming children with disabilities, there are no minimum training standards for general education teachers for special needs instruction. In teacher credential programs, prospective teachers may take a course on teaching special needs students, or programs may integrate special education topics into general education courses. Training for experienced teachers may be as minimal as one day of continuing education, if that. Fortunately, experienced teachers often can make effective adjustments to established strategies and techniques for guidance and discipline to support children with challenging issues. Other times, however, there is something special about the behavior or children's underlying energy that render "regular" responses ineffective. Children range from gifted to very challenged in a variety of ways: artistic skills, creativity, musical ability, auditory or visual comprehension, reading, physical coordination, abstract thinking, deductive versus inductive reasoning, and more. Sometimes there is an expectation for children to perform in the mid-range of expectations and abilities. Children who have challenges are often minimized, ignored, or deemed de facto negative. Society loses the benefit of their creativity and energy, "outside of the box" thinking, and revolutionary perspectives. If continually frustrated, children accrue stress, self-esteem deteriorates, and acting out increases. Temper tantrums and other disruptive behavior become habitual, leading to long-term social and emotional damages and academic and vocational failure. Conversely, well-supported children, recognized and supported for their strengths and trained to compensate for challenges, grow in self-esteem and social skills. They become more successful.

EXCLUSION . . . AND BULLYING

Children with challenges often process and behave similarly to, yet differently from, others. Children with any of the four challenges share an important characteristic: They are often identifiably different from other classmates. Without affirmative adult guidance, children's differences may activate problematic social dynamics, specifically exclusion and bullying. Bullying may be overtly physical, but also can manifest socially and relationally. Children's identified differences sometimes are difficult to handle or manage within the classroom. This is especially true if teachers don't understand them or are unclear how to attend to them. Understanding, respecting, celebrating, and accepting differences can lead to healthier classroom communities. On the other hand, ignorance and inexperience may lead to prejudice or worse: exclusion, sexism, racism, classism, bullyism (the practice of irrational force on a weak opponent or supposed weak opponent to exercise power), ablism (discrimination in favor of the able-bodied; asserting people with disabilities as being unable), and so forth. Otherwise well-intended teachers can promote inclusive philosophies yet may be unaware of harsh realities without greater understanding and guidance about how specific challenges affect children.

COMPROMISING THE INTENT OF INCLUSION

The challenge of inclusion is not always well met. Three practices can compromise the intent of inclusion. *Invisibility* is the practice of keeping people out of sight. Sometimes well-intended teachers downplay, ignore, or pretend not to notice disabilities or differences. They may fear causing others discomfort or embarrassment. Unfortunately, this implies that differences are unimportant. The totality of who I am is much more than just being an American-born son of Chinese immigrant parents. However, denying my experiences as a Chinese-American (born in 1953 during the Cold War, raised primarily in Berkeley, California, in a predominantly black neighborhood during the turbulent 1960s, and attending integrated schools from middle school to high school) would deny formative experiences that have significantly influenced who I am now. Denial or minimizing can happen with ethnic or religious differences as well as with learning ability, attention, restraint, social functioning, and other differences. Children with special needs need to be visible. Otherwise, they cannot become self-loving and self-reliant. They cannot learn how to handle bullies and other life circumstances. Teachers promote this by identifying and celebrating the range of diversity in all forms in the classroom, the greater communities, and the world. However, celebrating only differences can be uncomfortable and can cause children to be targeted for the differences. Instead, teachers can reveal and explore the range of diversity, including what may be assumed to be "normal."

Infantilizing also defeats self-reliance. Infantilizing is treating individuals with disabilities or differences as fundamentally incapable and dependent like infants. Consistent infantilizing messages create learned helplessness. Overprotected children "fulfill" low expectations of caring adults by becoming incapable, vulnerable, and dependent. Children with challenges often function quite well by drawing upon their strengths and developing compensations. Successful functioning happens only if they reach adulthood without debilitating emotional damage. While infants are expected to gradually develop greater abilities, infantilizing individuals keeps them unable. When teachers understand the depth, breadth, and nuances of any particular challenge, they can counter the presumption of inability. Teachers can then direct children to accentuate strengths and develop compensating abilities. Teachers and all adults support children by requiring them to take risks—to do the exploration and experimentation necessary to develop skills and strengths. Teachers should expect a lot, while providing guidance and support.

All people with differences or challenges possess many other abilities, traits, interests, and individual personalities. *Objectifying* causes harm by seeing only differences rather than whole individuals. When children are objectified, they become fundamentally limited by their definition as the label. For example, an African-American child should not be defined solely because of race. He or she is a child who has African-American ancestry and many additional attributes and experiences. Ethnicity or race probably has significant ramifications upon his or her emotional, psychological, and social processes, but not to the exclusion of other influences. In the same way, a child with LD can become characterized as a "learning-disabled child." That label implies he or she is predisposed to and functioning within some stereotypical spectrum of learning disabled behavior. Adults need to allow children to activate and develop in appropriate circumstances. Supporting children's diversity of skills and traits must be key principles in developmental and educational processes. Misunderstood, devalued, and frustrated, children with challenges become ostracized and misfits. Society loses their creativity, skills, energy, and other contributions.

CONTINUUMS OR LABELS

A label or diagnosis of having LD or being gifted, as opposed to serving to objectify a child, may activate or focus services or intervention. Understanding continuums allows for experience with "average" skilled children (the middle 68% in the two middle quadrants of a classic bell curve distribution) to aid diagnosis, intervention, and support for those on the higher and lower ranges (the highest 16% and the lowest 16%). Technical definitions by school districts or professional diagnosticians of what is considered a qualifying disability, disorder, or condition may be more restrictive than the 16% of each of the low and high ends of the bell curve quadrants. Such definitions are driven by a variety of circumstances and demands, including professional territoriality, educational, medical, legal, political, and not the least, financial considerations. Services that are activated by a diagnosis require expenditures of often-scarce financial resources. It is possible that children who need assistance and would otherwise qualify for a particular diagnosis might fail to receive the diagnosis. They could be designated as not extreme enough to warrant the diagnosis due to budgetary restrictions.

Each of the four major challenges discussed in this book deserves extensive study and review by educators, parents, and other adults working with children. There are numerous resources beyond those cited in this book in journals, books, and on Internet Web sites dedicated to understanding and supporting children with challenges. This book is not intended to be a comprehensive resource or for diagnosis on these challenges, although experienced teachers will likely recognize the children from the descriptions.

To begin acquiring more extensive information, readers may refer to the references at the end of the book.

THREE PERSPECTIVES

There are three perspectives in the book of which the reader should be aware. First, in the discussion about children with the four major challenges, there is always the risk of unintentionally stereotyping children individually or as a group. Despite great care in avoiding stereotyping, it may seem that I am trying to define a particular group of children, teachers, or parents. Please remember that theories and concepts, generalities and principles are meant to be supportive of teachers and other adults, so that they can better understand and then support individual children. What is the difference between a generality, principle, or theory versus a stereotype? What is the difference between prejudgment and bias? A generality, principle, or theory is generated from observations of large groups of individuals, experiences, or data. Interested professionals and citizens use the generality to aid them in understanding something or someone of concern. As a prejudgment, they have some expectation that who or what they are investigating will be comparable. As they find prejudgment applicable or not, it may serve them in their work. It becomes a stereotype or bias, however, when they expect what they are investigating will be same, despite any evidence to the contrary. It becomes destructive if they "see" what they are investigating only as the generality predicts. As some information in this book is applicable to a child or to children with whom the reader is working, it may be useful. If it is not applicable, it will not be useful. I cannot make that determination.

Second, the book focuses on children with challenges who become victimized regularly and children who habitually bully others. When there is discussion about children with a particular challenge who are victimized or are bullies, there is no intention to characterize all children with a particular challenge as being victims or bullies. The sad reality is that these children are often more vulnerable to gravitate toward these negative behaviors or circumstances. None of the challenges determines children's behaviors one way or another. Rather than blame victims or bullies, I assert that appropriate adult support or intervention can and should reduce such negative outcomes. Hopefully, the information in this book will help teachers and other adults understand how and why becoming perpetual victims or bullies may happen and how to keep it from happening. The book will discuss how children may have been disempowered and how to empower them.

Third, I intentionally use examples, research, and statistics from preschool ages through elementary school, but also from middle school, high school, and adulthood. The target population to be addressed in this book is young children. However, the use of various ages serves to emphasize that all of the issues discussed—LD, ADHD, AS, gifted abilities, victimization, bullying, social-emotional development, support and intervention, and so forth—either are lifelong issues or have potential to be lifelong issues. Being victimized or bullying also does not suddenly appear or disappear. Childhood experiences have great influence on whether individuals become powerful and healthy adults or become perpetual victims or bullies or other unhealthy adults. In addition, there are references to parent and family dynamics along with the focus on the classroom and school. The inclusion of information from a greater age span and of parent and family dynamics serves to emphasize that these issues are not isolated to early childhood or happen only at school. It infers a minimum need for information exchange between home and classroom. And it infers an optimal situation of full collaboration between parents and teachers to support children.

Chapter Highlights

- Principles of an inclusive classroom to address the challenges of learning and processing differences are similar to principles addressing socioeconomic diversities of race, ethnicity, religion, class, and family composition.

- The more teachers become aware of their knowledge, skills, and wisdom acquired working in the mainstream classroom with a familiar spectrum of child diversity, the more they can apply that to working with and supporting children with specific challenges.

- The more teachers become aware of their knowledge, skills, and wisdom acquired working with children with LD, ADHD, AS, and gifted abilities, the more they can apply that to working with and supporting a diversity of children in the mainstream classroom.

- Anything that interferes with or, conversely, supports emotional, psychological, or social stability affects children's readiness to learn and be taught.

- There always have been children with undiagnosed challenges in mainstream classrooms (especially, *that* kid in your classroom!), but now children with identified diagnoses are often placed into mainstream classrooms without additional or minimal educational support.

- Without affirmative adult guidance, children's differences may activate problematic social dynamics, specifically exclusion and bullying.

- Misunderstood, devalued, and frustrated, children with challenges become ostracized and misfits. Society loses their creativity, skills, energy, and other contributions.

- Understanding continuums allows for experience with "average" skilled children (the middle 68% in the two middle quadrants of a classic bell curve distribution) to aid diagnosis, intervention, and support for those on the higher and lower ranges (the highest 16% and the lowest 16%).

1

Inclusion, Exclusion, and Bullying

THE CHICKEN SPENDS ITS WHOLE LIFE . . .

The school and a student's mom asked me to consult about and to observe her four-year-old son, Eddie. She felt that another boy, Mitchell, was bullying him. The school officials were somewhat ambivalent about how much Eddie was being victimized. However, they admitted that something was going on. Eddie's days in preschool were not times of joyous exploration, social interaction, and academic stimulation. His calm immersion in playful exploration would be suddenly interrupted, as he caught a sudden movement or a discordant sound. "What's that? Is he coming this way?" he would say silently to himself when he saw Mitchell look his way. Trying as hard as he could to become invisible, he could tell that it was happening . . . again. "Please, not me again. How come not Billy? Or Juanita? Why me? Always me?" Anxiously, he looked for the teachers. No luck. One was by the sink helping clean a mess. The other was in the corner reading to a small group of kids. "They're not looking! Don't they know? Don't they see, it's happening again? Teacher! Mitchell's going to get me . . . again!" Mitchell was ready to "play" with Eddie. I had been watching unbeknownst to the children from outside the classroom door. I did not need to hear what was said. The body language and facial expressions of both Mitchell and Eddie communicated the bully and victim dance. I entered the room and caught Mitchell's eyes. He immediately disengaged from Eddie. Mitchell was smart enough to not only pick up on

Eddie's vulnerability, but also to scan the environment to see what he could get away with. An adult was watching. Eddie was "lucky" this time.

Eddie's family had experienced trauma previously, when a stray bullet shot by an unknown shooter had killed his father at the park. His mom was terrified that violence in the form of bullying had found her family again. Were they doomed? Were they somehow attracting violence? She anguished, "Why is my son targeted by this new bully?"

> Targets for harassment can be chosen for any number of reasons. They aren't necessarily victims nor do they necessarily seek or need acceptance from the bully's peer group. Simply being a newcomer to a school without immediate friends or alliances might be enough to draw a bully's attention. A perceived slight, a manner of dress or deportment, association with a disliked peer or relative, or even success in school could be reason enough for one person to bully another. On the other hand, bullies become emboldened if they sense that a potential target is vulnerable. (Parsons, 2003, p. 45)

When I initially went to observe, no one pointed out either the supposed victim, Eddie, or the supposed bully, Mitchell. I didn't immediately identify Mitchell as the bully, but I easily recognized the "victim" among the twenty children in the classroom. Any bully could have picked Eddie out among the children as the "One." In my psychotherapy practice, an adult client, KC, felt she was, from early childhood, the one always picked on. Since childhood, bad things always seemed to happen to her, the favored victim for the world's bullies. Anguished, she cried out,

> Why always me? How do they find me? The other night . . . I went to dinner with my grandma. Waiting for a table, we ordered wine and sat at a small table in the bar. There I was . . . baggy sweats, hair in a ponytail, no makeup . . . minding my own business. Out of the corner of my eye . . . or, maybe I heard a tone . . . or, some kind of sixth sense . . . I looked up and there in the doorway was . . . trouble!

How did KC know with just one look that he was trouble? She knew because the chicken spends its whole life learning how to recognize the hawk. Children who are bullied, victimized, or picked on from early on or throughout childhood often learn quickly to recognize their predators, the bullies. The experience of KC was not an isolated adult incident, but a continuation of childhood traumas. At one time, KC had been the "Eddie" to the bullies in her childhood. And she was still the "one" to adult bullies in adulthood.

A classroom cannot just throw children together and assume a cohesive community will result. Inclusion puts children with others who may have aggressive to toxic emotional or behavioral energy—bullies or "mean" kids. Unfortunately, teachers, parents, and other adults can hold an illusion of childhood, classrooms, and playgrounds as idyllic sanctuaries of warm, loving innocence. They deny the existence and actions of bullies or mean kids. They then fail to anticipate or prepare children to deal with such realities. Children with special needs may come from compassionate, nurturing, and protective environments supervised by conscientiously dedicated adults. In other words, they initially grow up in a loving sanctuary without harshness and mean kids. Or the adult management had been so vigilant that otherwise problematic interactions are nipped in the bud or resolved by adult interventions. Unfortunately, such adult intervention does not empower children to care for themselves. If overprotected, some children do not learn how to protect themselves from aggression. Children with processing issues may have trouble recognizing the predatory children. Other children with distraction issues may not perceive warning cues. Still other children may note cues but misinterpret them. After repeated experiences of being picked on or bullied without sufficient recourse and support, victimized individuals may learn to recognize perpetrators. They may become hypervigilant and hypersensitive to any potential interaction, threatening or benign. Feeling vulnerable, unable to protect themselves, their only hope becomes to recognize the predator before it attacks and hopefully avoid it. Eddie and my client KC had both become hypersensitive and hypervigilant to anticipate potential abusers. Unfortunately, hypersensitivity and hypervigilance were not only ineffective, but increased the probability of harassment.

THE HAWK SPENDS ITS WHOLE LIFE . . .

KC had seen him before—not him specifically, but bullies like him back in elementary school, just as Eddie experienced bullies in his preschool. She saw them later in middle and high school, and eventually, at work, in social situations—everywhere. She had met bullies all her life. With a glint in his eyes, the smirk, and the body posture, the hawk had found her again. A tremor crept into her voice:

> I turned away quickly to avoid eye contact! Out of the corner of my eye, I watched . . . standing with hands on hips. Scanning the room . . . and, then he walked right up to me! And started messing with me! Why me out of all those women in the room? A dozen others . . . some dressed up . . . pretty makeup . . . some sitting alone! Why not them? But he came up to me! How do they always know that I'm the one? The easiest to abuse?

Predatory individuals seek power and control over others, but carefully aggress against the weakest or most vulnerable. Any individual (particularly, any child) identifiably different becomes a potential target for bullies. If children's vulnerabilities are not mitigated through a process of empowerment, they risk continuing to be prey to bullies for decades as KC had been. Being special or gifted distinguishes individuals as different and thus potential victims. Once victimized, a cycle of vulnerability may build upon itself. Thoughtful teachers are wary that greater diversity in classrooms does not result in greater exclusion and bullying. They are adamant and assertive that any bullying is unacceptable. Unfortunately, some adults accept and implicitly condone such aggression as "kids being kids." Or they may give gender permission by accepting that "boys will be boys" or all female socialization is innocent. The classic novel, *Lord of the Flies* (Golding, 1954), where shipwrecked schoolboys without adult guidance descend into barbaric murder reminds us of how boys can be! Exclusion from cliques is a painful memory for many women. Effective teachers consistently set clear boundaries and consistently follow through with clear consequences about hurtful behavior. Then boys and girls will be citizens in healthy communities—first, the classroom and later in society.

For example, teachers may need to help children understand and respect the special name that his or her parent chose through a lesson on names and meanings from different cultures. For many children, having what others may call a special quality does not result in them feeling special in any positive way. They may feel they don't belong because of their special challenges or capacities. If they become marginal members on the periphery of the social group, they become like the crippled deer on the edge of the herd. The wolf pack targets them. Abusers know individuals with higher status, confidence, and social-emotional and peer resources (friends) can and will resist and fight back. Bullies leave them alone as too much trouble to mess with. This is especially true if there is easy prey they can pick on or exclude without objection from the community.

The life of the victim is a miserable existence. Glew, Fan, Katon, Rivara, and Kernic (2005) reported in their study of over 3,000 third-, fourth-, and fifth-grade students that "only 42% of students defined as victims and 44% of those defined as bully-victims said that they had reported their victimization to someone" (p. 1026). When not being picked on, they worry if and when they will be picked on again. There were not any places at school that seemed safe, including those with adult supervision. "The playground was the most likely site (71%) for victimization followed by classrooms (46%), gym classes (40%), lunchrooms (39%), halls and stairs (33%), and buses (28%)" (p. 1026). Paraprofessionals, parent volunteers, or teachers' aides often supervise the playground where most of the abuse occurs. Unfortunately that may mean that the least trained and aware of bully and victim dynamics, including playground supervisors who may be the least aware of problematic students from not having observed classrooms, are witnesses to most of the events. Teacher scrutiny and intervention on the playground may be more important than classroom supervision. Children may experience both vulnerability to being bullied and vulnerability caused by being bullied.

> Being bullied frequently is likely to be a considerable source of stress. Depression among those who were frequently bullied might be expected. However, adolescents who are depressed may also

attract negative attention from their peers. Previous research suggests that compared with their peers, those who are bullied are more introverted, less assertive, and are overinvolved in their families. Victims also tend to be rejected by peers. Depression could thus be both a result of and a reason for being bullied. (Kaltiala-Heino, Rimpelä, Marttunen, Rimpelä, & Rantanen, 1999, p. 350)

Being victimized or exhibiting consequences of victimization doesn't always draw empathy or support. People may begin to avoid victims. They can become more isolated in their communities: the office, playground, classroom, and family. Unrecognized consequences from extreme stress may occur in additional to emotional, psychological, social, or academic consequences. In a study of 15,686 students (including 8,370 girls) in Grades 6 through 10, "girls who experienced bullying at least once a week were more likely to experience headaches, backaches, and morning fatigue compared with girls who had not been bullied during that term" (Ghandour, Overpeck, Huang, Kogan, & Scheidt, 2004, p. 801). Some children come to hate or fear going to the school (school phobia). Somatic problems may develop: stomachaches, headaches, or other maladies so Mommy or Daddy keeps them home. Social phobia (fear of social situations) or agoraphobia (fear of leaving the house) may develop. People, even close friends, teachers, and parents may get frustrated or even angry with depressed individuals, resulting in subtle and not-so-subtle messages implying something is wrong with them as victims. Eventually they believe something must be wrong about them; often what is special about them is what is "wrong." When teachers and other adults recognize that being a victim can result in a victim personality, there is less likelihood of pathologizing, that is, blaming the victim.

ANXIOUS VULNERABILITY

Victimized children are often younger than their bullies. They tend to be more naturally sensitive, cautious, quiet, and anxious, tend to have negative views of violence, and are fairly nonaggressive in interactions. Physical weakness (youth or size) and anxiety potentially targets them. Relational and physical traits alone, however, are not predictive of being victimized. As opposed to sensitive, healthy, nonvictimized children, victims tend to withdraw from confrontations of any kind and respond to confrontations (attacks) with crying. Faced with conflict, they become paralyzed with fear. Children with gifted or mature intellectual abilities may understand logical and appropriate behavior, but be unable to comprehend other's impulsive behavior. Short-term gratification resulting in long-term negative consequences doesn't make sense to them. Nor do they understand the complex emotional and psychological motivations for bullies' aggression. This may cause them confusion in how to respond. Children with LD or AS may misinterpret cues that reveal aggressive mood changes. This can result in being surprised and feeling ambushed. Eventually, some children may exhibit an "anxious vulnerability." Easily recognized by bullies, it is as if floating over their heads were flashing signs broadcasting, "Attention: Victim here!" Once children feel that they can do nothing if bullies attack them, then avoidance of bullies is their only defensive strategy. By being hypervigilant and constantly scanning the environment, such children hope to see the bullies before they get too close to strike. Victims also must become hypersensitive to any sound, movement, expression, or energy that potentially could be indicative of an attack. Guessing incorrectly and moving away or otherwise avoiding innocuous play invitations and social interactions becomes a common response. Such children prefer erring and wasting energy and losing opportunities for play and friendship, rather than missing an impending attack and getting annihilated. Getting immersed in any activity because it is fascinating, exciting, or fun is to be avoided because it would cause them to lose their alertness and become vulnerable to an ambush. Such children show anxious vulnerability even in nonconflict situations. With his anxious vulnerability, his rabbit eyes and nervous energy, Eddie had internalized the trauma, loss, and fear that he and his mother experienced with his father's murder. Tense and hypervigilant, Eddie inadvertently broadcast to the predator that he was the easy prey to attack.

PLEASE PLEASE PLEASE . . .

Victim personalities' approach to conflict is often passive (with important exceptions to be discussed later regarding the bully-victim or reactive bully). Unassertive, victims tend not to try to negotiate and make few or no demands, requests, or suggestions. They hope that things will get better ("please please please . . ."). Since they don't "make their luck," their reality often is miserable. They don't initiate interactions. They tend to be passive in play. Despite other developmental maturity beyond appropriate parallel play (three and under), they continue to play next to rather than with others. They are often socially incompetent, but not aggressive or antisocial. Often unable to handle aggression alone, they need to be rescued. Adult rescue or intervention, however, can backfire on everyone. Children who are victimized and then rescued do not need to and subsequently fail to learn how to manage or problem solve aggression against them. In addition, adult rescue confirms these children's victim identity of being inherently helpless in the face of aggression. Ongoing victimization is often a consequence of adult failures to give empowering support. Victims feel worse and worse, ever more anxious, which increases their "anxious vulnerability," leading to further victimization. They are submissive in the face of aggression, which rewards bullies' egos. Bullies continually return to them for further satisfaction, rather than seek new targets. Despite being told to avoid bullies, victims seem to gravitate to them anyway. Bullies and victims coexist at the bottom of the social hierarchy. Victims often become socially isolated, so needy for attention that negative attention from association with bullies can become desirable over no attention at all.

Adults must intervene when circumstances are overwhelming or too dangerous for children to handle alone. It may be beyond their developmental capacities, emotionally, socially, or cognitively. Or simple boundaries will not suffice because of the intensity, relentlessness, or insidious creativity of the abusers. Children in these cases will be greatly challenged to succeed and may try and still fail. However, when adults step in immediately, they steal children's opportunities to struggle successfully, or to fail, but survive. Children need encouragement, training, and empowerment from adults, *and* for them to let go appropriately. Only then can children struggle and suffer to build necessary skills and resiliency to handle stress, conflicts, and intrusive or abusive or exploitative people. Adults need to gauge specific situations guided by the basic principles of empowerment through doing as little as possible and only as much as needed. Whatever adults do in terms of interventions, children do not have to do or learn. Here is an example of an adult's minimal intervention, with significant guidance and empowerment, from my book, *The One-Minute Temper Tantrum Solution* (2008, p. 106). This passage is about judiciously intervening with a small child who felt helpless when a bully took his bucket. Each progressive step comes with an assessment of how much support is needed. At any given step, if the child can complete the process, the adult does not and must not continue intervening.

Jordan, that little girl took your bucket. You don't look happy. Is that okay? No? Take it back. Little girl, Jordan wants to talk to you. Don't go away. Jordan, get your bucket. Get your bucket . . . Mommy won't get it for you. You need to get it. She'll give it back to you.

[A firm glance at her would be useful here!]

Tell her, "No."

[If Jordan can successfully take it from here, let him do it. If he can't, then ask the following question.]

You need help? Here she is. Put your hand on the bucket. Hold on.

[If Jordan can successfully take it from here, let him do it. If he can't, then ask the following question.]

Okay? Now, pull it away.

[If necessary, close your hand around his hand on the bucket.]

There you go! You did it! Good job, you got your bucket. What do you want to do with your bucket now? You want to put sand in it? You want to let her play with it? Or play together with her? You decide.

Empowerment is the key to keeping children from becoming perpetual victims. The very first step is determining whether a child like Jordan needs any assistance at all. If he can take care of himself and his bucket, then adults should do *nothing!* Adults need to find whatever strength or skills a child may have. Even if the strength or skills are somewhat minuscule, adults can build upon them. If a child already has a sense of power and control, then adult monitoring and possible guidance would be based on how appropriate the response may be. Hitting, for example, would not be OK. If the child is not able or is hesitant in dealing with the aggression, then the first step in the empowerment process is to acknowledge the issues and the child's needs. Saying it out loud, so that the transgressor hears it, sets the context and requirement for both Jordan and the other child. Observe if Jordan can get the bucket back without further guidance. If yes, great! Affirm Jordan's act of self-care! If Jordan isn't able to act or doesn't know how to act, then the adult provides language: "Tell her, 'No!'" Observe if Jordan can proceed successfully from this. If yes, great! Affirm Jordan's act of self-care! If not, then provide more but limited guidance or assistance.

If Jordan refuses or is otherwise unable to complete the necessary behavior, the adult should complete the process, including disciplining the other child as is appropriate, so as not to reward the other child his or her aggression. However, the adult should also not reward Jordan for failing to take care of himself. In this scenario, that would mean get the bucket back, but not to give it to Jordan. This may sound harsh or uncaring, but getting the bucket back is not as important as the potential lesson. A child like Jordan needs to learn that his action or inaction creates the consequences of his life. Passive inaction cannot be rewarded through adult rescuing. Both Eddie and KC had to be supported, guided, and required to confront their bullies. With Eddie, teachers set the situation up for him to confront Mitchell. They monitored the interaction so that it would not get out of control. However, they did not confront Mitchell *for* Eddie. Eddie was able to gradually become more competent at standing up for himself or asking for help if necessary. This growth took a fair amount of teacher energy and several weeks, but Eddie became practiced and empowered. Mitchell learned that Eddie wasn't an easy victim anymore. He had learned to tell Mitchell, "No!" and to report Mitchell if necessary. KC's process was essentially the same but done through therapy and coaching her through life challenges. She talked about her original vulnerability as a child and how she was victimized. KC was able to recognize that she had power as an adult that she had never had before, and she began asserting her power. She set boundaries and applied consequences to others depending on how they treated her. As she became more effective, her confidence grew, gradually replacing anxious vulnerability. When the predators scanned the room for easy victims, she no longer stood out.

THE LOUD AGGRESSIVE "VICTIM" BECOMES A BULLY

Some children become reactive bullies, also known as bully-victims. They are ineffective aggressors who get the worst of being both bullies and victims. Rather than passively accepting powerlessness, these children may assert loudly, aggressively, or violently their victimization. They may justify their own aggressive behavior as retaliation against others. "What did you expect me to do? I had to hit him!" Ineffective bullies, unable to be socially successful with other children, get stuck associating with other bullies, including more dominating bullies. Since they are often very insecure being in the bully social group, they are easily provoked. Unable to calm down, they escalate minor incidents into aggressive situations. They may make threatening comments or gestures. The more powerful and intimidating alpha bullies provoke, threaten, and intimidate them back. Since they know the more aggressive bullies can and will bring greater violence into an actual confrontation, they get overwhelmed by them and feel forced to back down. The cross-cultural research of Nansel et al. (2004) found severe consequences for the bully-victim.

> The most striking pattern of psychosocial adjustment was demonstrated by the bully-victims, who reported levels of emotional adjustment, relationships with classmates, and health problems similar to those of victims, with levels of school adjustment and alcohol use similar to those of bullies. Moreover, in some cases, their scores were significantly worse than those of either bullies or victims. In 8 countries bully-victims reported more health problems than the other 2 groups, and in 5 countries they reported more school adjustment problems. (p. 734)

Bully-victims have the highly negative social consequences of the bully (antisocial behavior, poor academics, crime, and so forth), and the internalized negative consequences of the victim (anxiety and depression). More powerful and aggressive bullies repeatedly provoke them because of their highly emotional responses. Other bullies subjectively experience benefits with gains of power and control and possible social status from their behavior. Reactive bullies are actually ineffective at gaining these benefits! With a growing sense of powerlessness, resentment, and domination by more powerful bullies, reactive bullies become increasingly likely to victimize others, be oppositional, defiant, and passive-aggressive.

Adults may not recognize that reactive bullies have core emotional experiences like classic victims. As a result, adult boundaries and consequences for their bullying activities accentuate reactive bullies' already existing feelings of victimization. Their feelings of victimization, unlike as for other children, don't draw any real compassion from adults. These children may be more prone to developing increasingly resentful victimization or paranoid feelings. Reactive bullies need especially skilled adults to manage the balance between validating their feelings of victimization while setting appropriate boundaries against their aggressive behaviors. They need to be given specific instructions how to express frustration and gain healthy power and control without resorting to aggression. For example, "I know you feel it's unfair, and you will not get what you want by hitting." The energy to seek more power and control can be acknowledged as a strength that is exerted ineffectively. The choice, "You can make it better or make it worse," becomes a reminder of the power and control children have in their lives. Reactive bullies and many other children need to be reminded that they often make their lives worse with their choices. "Screaming at them doesn't make them like you better. It makes them really dislike you." They need repeated reframing of what they perceive as their dire circumstances to realize that they are not helpless. "You're not happy with this. If you quit, you make it worse. If you talk to me, you might make it better. You choose." They also need clear alternatives to the aggressive behaviors they assert they have to do. Tell them, specifically, do this, say this, and so forth. If teachers can see through the whining and bullying behavior, they may be able to find the compassion to support reactive bullies.

VICTIM ENTITLEMENT TO BULLY AND INTELLECTUAL BULLYING

Reactive bullies, like some overwhelmed or victimized children, may develop a sense of entitlement to be spiteful and vindictive. They can accrue gigantic reservoirs of resentments and grievances. Family members, teachers, or other children become targets. For example, a child with LD or ADHD may load up with negative feedback at school and, as a result, throw tantrums at home. Academically gifted but unfulfilled by schoolwork, a child may sneer when her mother asks if she has any homework. A child with AS, excluded by classmates, may cruelly tease and manipulate his younger sibling in turn. Any of these behaviors will draw further reprimands, negative feedback, and problematic social consequences. If the consequences are experienced as being unfair, they further reinforce frustration and resentment. Cycles of aggression must be interrupted, if not by children's actions, then through adult or classroom intervention.

Children may attempt intellectual aggression, while asserting other people are stupid or that their actions justify verbal assaults. Adults need to recognize the "invitation" to engage in the fruitless debate and name the disrespect. They need to assert clear boundaries and consequences not only about overt verbal insults, but also about heavy sighs, rolling the eyes, smacking lips, blank stares, and other passive-aggressive nonverbal communications. Teachers can acknowledge that children are trying to make a point and that they want to hear it. They can give feedback that the communication style is ineffective. "My attention is drawn mostly to your tone, instead of what you're trying to say. Please, tell me same thing in a more respectful tone, so I can hear it." With this statement, the boundaries are asserted without being drawn into a fruitless argument. Often a direct confrontation about disrespectful passive-aggressive behavior draws outrage. "Whaaat!? What'd I do!? I didn't do nuthin'!"

Passive-aggressiveness gives individuals the illusion of power and control. Unfortunately, it also precludes them from learning how to develop appropriate means to gain true power and control. Aggressors seldom realize that they trigger the ensuing resentment, exclusion, or negative treatment by others. Healthy and successful life and relationships are severely compromised with cycles of interpersonal communication that include passive-aggressive behavior. Teachers can best reach passive-aggressive individuals by avoiding getting caught up in the moral or inferiority versus superiority argument. Focusing on everyone's relative roles and requirements in the situation may help. "Whether you're right or wrong, or everyone is stupid, you cannot scream in class." They should constantly refocus children on the functional result of their being so adamant. "Even though you're sure you're right, you won't get what you want." Sometimes when their self-righteous arousal is intense, none of this will work. It is best not to cycle over and over with the same arguments. Instead, set a boundary and consequence, and follow through immediately. If there is outrage and further attempts to continue the argument, then prompt, "You make it better or make it worse. Continuing to argue will make it worse. Cooperating will make it better. You choose." Children best learn about their power and control in life when adults assert clear boundaries and clear consequences. When adults allow passive-aggressive children to keep them in an argument, the children feel they are in control.

CLASSIFICATION CREATES TARGETS FOR EXCLUSION

A respectful classroom is more than promoting acceptance and "niceness." Children who are victimized often find that being nice doesn't protect them from bullies. Reactive bullies often forget about being nice when they feel victimized. Bullies can be nice, but sometimes their need to dominate and intimidate is much stronger. Teachers encourage students to accept everyone as the same, but discover students notice differences in the "same as themselves" children. Pretending everyone is the same disrespects the uniqueness of individuals. Ignorance leads to assumptions that differences are "bad." And bad things or people get punished. Classmates may punish others with exclusion from friendships, games, and activities. Exclusion or being ostracized extends to the playground and beyond. It may be the first step toward even more severe aggression. Throughout history, individuals, religions, races, communities, or groups ("those people" or "them") have been classified as different and then targeted for abuse or exclusion to serve individual, social, or political agendas. Stanton (1998) names classification and dehumanization as keys, along with denial, to genocide. While genocide is a societal act upon another group, abuse and bullying are the acts of individuals or a group upon others. Teachers set the tone about differences, inclusion, aggression, victimization, and bullying. Children want to get along with each other. They want to belong. They want to be liked, including by teachers. Teachers are the guardians of the classroom community and must activate these positive energies to create a respectful community. Teacher silence about bullying gives permission for children to be victimized. Teacher communication and action takes that permission away.

Chapter Highlights

- Children who are bullied, victimized, or picked on from early on or throughout childhood often learn quickly to recognize their predators, the bullies.

- Predatory individuals seek power and control over others, but carefully aggress against the weakest or most vulnerable. Any individual, particularly any child, identifiably different becomes a potential target for bullies.

- Some children come to hate or fear going to the school (school phobia). Somatic problems may develop: stomachaches, headaches, or other maladies so Mommy or Daddy keeps them home. Social phobia (fear of social situations) or agoraphobia (fear of leaving the house) may develop.

- Eventually, some children may exhibit an "anxious vulnerability." Easily recognized by bullies, it is as if floating over their heads were flashing signs broadcasting, "Attention: Victim here!"

- Adults need to gauge specific situations guided by the basic principles of empowerment through doing as little as possible and only as much as needed. Whatever adults do in terms of interventions, children do not have to do or learn.

- Ineffective bullies, unable to be socially successful with other children, get stuck associating with other bullies, including more dominating bullies.

- With growing sense of powerlessness, resentment, and domination by more powerful bullies, reactive bullies become increasingly likely to victimize others, be oppositional, defiant, and passive-aggressive.

- Some overwhelmed or victimized children may develop a sense of entitlement to be spiteful and vindictive.

- As self-righteous aggression without overt verbal or physical attacks, passive-aggressiveness gives individuals the illusion of power and control. Unfortunately, it also precludes them learning how to develop appropriate means to gain true power and control.

- A respectful classroom is more than promoting acceptance and "niceness."

2

The Stress, Frustrate, Fail, Suffer *Method and Emotional Intelligence*

THE REAL WORLD

A sea of mostly expectant faces turned toward me. It was a parent education night for a pricey preschool program. All of the parents had invested heavily, financially and emotionally, in their children's development. They were now investing time this evening to hear more about what they could do to ensure their children's success and happiness. After a flowery introduction by the director, I took the lectern. I said, "There's one thing I need to tell you. Despite everything you have done, do, and will do for your children, you need to know that . . . your children are *not* special!" There were gasps of surprise, open mouths . . . and some smiles, laughter, and knowing glances between couples. I was playfully making hamburger out of a sacred cow! I continued:

> Of course, they're special to you . . . you're their parents! Nothing is more special than children to parents. Well, the teachers know they're special, but they have a whole room full of children who are

special. In the classroom, little Jamie isn't so special that he gets to be the line leader every day. Maria isn't so special that the other kids immediately relinquish to her the toys they're playing with. Loving parents and caring teachers need to prepare children for the real world where most people won't think of them as much less treat them as if they're special. And, unfortunately, as your children grow older there will be fewer people and less energy spent looking for the specialness in your children. So the challenge becomes, "How do you prepare your children for the real world?"

Parents often give their children a second chance, a third chance, and a fourth chance and more . . . because they're special! But can individuals count on those repeated chances in the real world? No matter how obnoxious their children's behavior, parents still love them. Can teachers always do that when their classrooms are in chaos from repeated disruptive behavior? Can students in the classroom count on getting others' affection, due consideration, or flexibility? Will classmates and teachers adapt to their needs and nuances? Parents often let their children win games because they get so upset when they lose. In the classroom, can these children deal with failure? Later, when they apply to colleges, can they deal with rejection? Disappointment is a part of the real world. Winning or losing a simple game may ignite huge differences in mood. Does the real world tolerate such moods? Children with the challenges highlighted in this book may be less equipped for the real world. Unfortunately, the people of the real world may not have any desire, understanding, or compassion for individuals with challenges and would put little if any effort into helping them bring their performance up to the others' standards.

For their emotional and psychological health, you need to disappoint children: specifically to stress them; allow frustration and failure; and let them suffer while experiencing stress, frustration, and failure! Teachers play critical roles in this process. They are often the first to begin to hold children up to the requirements of the real world. The classroom contrasts with the family world, with its smaller adult-child ratios. Teachers have to enforce real world demands among a whole classroom of children. Teachers who truly treasure the uniqueness of each child will adapt and flex support and instruction to individual needs. However, they cannot individualize and treat each child as special the way parents can. Fortunately, one of the major goals of early childhood education is to integrate children as equal members of the classroom community. Good teaching and parenting seek to develop powerful children who achieve a healthy balance between individuality and a sense of community. The letters *SFFS SS SS SF* are a mnemonic I developed to represent the process for building powerful and successful children.

THE FIRST *S* IS FOR *STRESS*—STRESS 'EM!

Stress does not destroy people, although unremitting stress can be destructive. Robert Sapolsky (2005), professor of biological sciences, explained a multitude of negative neurological and physical consequences from constant stress. The ability to deal successfully with stress defines one's ability to be successful. Avoiding stress avoids opportunities to learn how to successfully deal with it. Disappointment is a regular part of life. Is it fair that one child has challenges and another doesn't? Whether fair or not, the fact remains that a child has a challenge. Rather than obsessing about disappointments and limitations, children need to accept life's unfairness. Acceptance enables them to progress to affirmative struggles to seize available power and control for life. Having LD, ADHD, AS, or being gifted brings stresses to children. However, being an oppressed minority in an intolerant society is stressful too . . . or being female in a sexist society. Stressed barely begins to describe growing up with abusive parents. Many historically respected and influential individuals struggled with stress and trauma and achieved character, wisdom, and greatness as a result. The Serenity Prayer, commonly attributed to Reinhold Niebuhr, asks for one to be granted "the serenity to accept the things I cannot change; courage to change the things I can; and wisdom to know the difference." It does not ask to be stress-free!

THE FIRST *F* IS FOR *FRUSTRATION*—FRUSTRATE 'EM!

Stress often leads to frustration. Perseverance and success despite frustration develop the greatest self-esteem, sense of potency, and mastery. Handling frustration is critical to maturity. Children with LD are often frustrated with academic challenges that others grasp easily. Children with ADHD are frustrated when others impede their impulsivity and hyperactivity. Missing social cues, getting teased, and difficulty in making friends frustrate children with AS. Children with gifted abilities often are frustrated when others don't understand what is so obvious to them. Despite frustration that often is especially severe for children with challenges, the next question needs to be, "And now what?" If children expect things to be easy, challenges make them feel doomed and helpless. They may become infuriated at themselves, others, and anyone or anything else in their community unfortunate to be within striking distance. Adults need to let children experience frustration and let them know that they will be available to guide them, while requiring them to manage it appropriately. Adults need to place children in situations that will be challenging or difficult for them. Then they can prompt children with, "And now what are you going to do next?"

F IS FOR *FAILURE*—LET 'EM FAIL! (MAKE SURE THEY FAIL!)

Life is often about tremendous frustration *and* devastating failure! Teachers and other adults need to let children experience failure. No one strikes gold 100% of the time. To be successful, people need to be comfortable with failure or the possibility of failure. To fail and persevere and become successful reflects resiliency. When adults manipulate circumstances to make it easy, children will assume that success is the norm. The other kid on the playground isn't going to let them win the race, much less another candidate let them have the job! Academic work might be easy for some children who are gifted. Despite visual disabilities, other children may have accompanying auditory processing strengths that allow excellence recognizing musical complexity. Running is easy for some children with ADHD. The intense concentration characteristic of children with AS may allow them to produce assignments much quicker than their classmates. On the other hand, all children experience failure, and children with challenges often experience much more failure. A child's ADHD energy can disrupt sedate times in the classroom. The intense concentration of AS may make it difficult for a child to focus on what the teacher actually wants. A child with gifted mathematical abilities produces the correct answer, but doesn't show the requested step-by-step calculations the teacher requires. Other children with gifted abilities may become perfectionists who are intolerant of less than excellence. They may label themselves as failures for not already knowing or being great at something just introduced. Learning to embrace failure or accepting performance short of perfection may be particularly challenging for some children with gifted abilities.

> The key to success is failing. So asserted Nathan Levy, an education consultant with expertise in gifted education. All students—and especially gifted children—need to learn that they will "fail, fail, fail until they succeed," the former teacher and administrator told his workshop audience (at the 2000 ASCD Annual Conference). Teachers, said Levy, need to give students real problems that they must struggle with and, perhaps, not immediately solve. "We need to build an environment where kids aren't afraid to fail," he stated. And students "need to learn to support each other, to say, 'Don't worry, I messed up last time, and it's no big deal.'" (Checkley, 2003, p. 7)

Let them fail? Make sure they fail! But doesn't it already happen too much for children with challenges? Perhaps, but it's still necessary. As strange as it sounds, adults need to celebrate failure! "Messed up? Awesome! Let's see how many times it takes before you get it!" Without failure, there is no success. "You got it! You kept on trying even when you failed over and over. Great!"

THE SECOND *S* IS FOR *SUFFER*—LET 'EM SUFFER!

Suffering is another unavoidable experience of living in the real world. Stress, frustration, and failure can cause intense emotional reactions, including depression, anxiety, fear, pain, rejection, abandonment, hurt, and shame. Adults must let children suffer. "Yes, it will be hard, and you can still do it." "No, it doesn't feel good, and you can still be OK." If teachers or other adults let children suffer, they are asserting confidence that children can handle it. Children who may not yet have the confidence that they will be OK depend on that confidence in them. Rescuing them from suffering or preventing them from experiencing suffering is often an automatic instinct of caring adults. Children will always eventually experience things that cause emotional distress regardless of how much adults try to protect or rescue them. Suffering cannot be prevented, but can be managed to prevent debilitation and paralysis. As with stress, frustration, and failure, only experience and practice with suffering develop emotional intelligence skills.

EMOTIONAL INTELLIGENCE

Psychologists, evolutionary biologists, psychiatrists, computer scientists, and others have described human capacities involved in identifying and understanding emotions. Daniel Goleman (1995), in *Emotional Intelligence,* popularized the concept to the general public. Emotional intelligence improves social effectiveness and social relations. Individuals with high emotional intelligence are less likely to engage in problem behaviors, and they avoid self-destructive, negative behaviors, or aggressive conflicts with others. Mayer, Caruso, and Salovey (1999) define emotional intelligence as follows:

> Emotional intelligence refers to an ability to recognize the meanings of emotion and their relationships, and to reason and problem-solve on the basis of them. Emotional intelligence is involved in the capacity to perceive emotions, assimilate emotion-related feelings, understand the information of those emotions, and manage them. (p. 267)

Mayer and Salovey (1997, p. 11) organized emotional intelligence into four different areas according to the nature of the abilities they examined. Each of these areas when applied to children with LD, ADHD, AS, or giftedness offers insight to their specific challenges.

1. *Perceiving Emotion.* Facial expressions such as happiness, sadness, anger, and fear are universally recognizable in and by human beings. The ability to accurately perceive the emotional content of facial expressions or

voice tone or inflections of others is critical to understanding of emotions, and thus the thinking and intentions of others. "Individuals who cannot empathize with others' feelings are less likely to curb their own aggression, and more likely to become insensitive to brutality in general" (Wallach, 1994, p. 3). Children with LD or ADHD may have typical or even high emotional intelligence but may become low functioning as their visual or auditory processing or distractibility causes them to miss emotional cues. A fundamental characteristic of children with AS is trouble interpreting social cues, which compromises their ability to perceive others' emotions. High emotional intelligence is not the same as high cognitive ability or IQ.

> Having a high IQ does not necessarily mean that a child will have high levels of emotional intelligence. A gifted child can have high, moderate, or low levels of it. . . . Gifted children who have low levels of emotional intelligence are at risk of social or emotional problems. . . . At the other end of the spectrum, gifted children with high levels of emotional intelligence may have difficulty managing the intensity and complexity of their feelings. They can be overwhelmed by their emotions unless they are in supportive environments that help them develop competence in understanding, interpreting, and coping with their feelings. (Emotional Intelligence, 2002, Emotional Intelligence and Gifted Children section, ¶ 1)

The spectrum of low to high emotional intelligence varies significantly among children with different challenges. Their emotions and behaviors may especially confuse teachers and other adults without experience with such children.

2. *Using Emotions to Facilitate Thought.* Emotions may be important for certain kinds of creativity to emerge. Unfortunately, the overriding emotions for children with challenges may be frustration, hurt, sadness, anxiety, and anger. Rejection and abandonment fears become prioritized emotions because of frequent victimization. Rather than facilitate thinking, emotions obscure thinking that could otherwise lead to functional choices for long-term success. Frustration from academic failures for children with ADHD or LD may prompt thoughts about avoiding schoolwork rather than how to do better. Depression and anxiety about social difficulties for children with AS may cause them to obsess about incurring classmates' dislike, rather than making good choices. Some children with gifted abilities tend to have very intense emotions (called overexcitability), which confuse rather than clarify thinking.

3. *Understanding Emotions.* Emotions convey critical information to others. Happiness has a logical set of messages and behaviors, while sadness has another set. If individuals feel deceived or taken advantage of,

anger is a likely emotion. Anger also comes with predictable actions: aggressive behavior, vengeance, reaching out, or calming behaviors such as reading or physical release. Individuals with high emotional intelligence tend to understand emotional messages and associated actions. They can reason with emotions and about emotions. Thus, they may be better able to accept both themselves and other people. Children with challenges are often frustrated and react in ways that neither they nor adults understand. "Why did you do that?" becomes an unanswerable question. It is an accusatory rhetorical question that can trigger conflicting thoughts and feelings. Since it is in the form of a question, children try to find a response to please adults. This attempt can cause anxiety since they sense adults' disapproval or frustration. Adults need to refrain from using rhetorical questions such as "Why did you do that?" They are accusations to children that they did something wrong. Worse, a rhetorical question asserts that the child did something incomprehensible, that no well-behaved, sensible, intelligent, or normal child would do! The rhetorical question doesn't even ask if the child did it or not. Children feel compelled to come up with an answer to the rhetorical question. They don't have sufficient insight or language to articulate, "I did that because . . .

- I was frustrated other kids shouted out the answer before I could figure it out [characteristic of a memory retrieval learning disability]. Now I'm upset, and needing some sense of mastery; I got it by bothering Suzie!"
- when I'm excited my body moves faster than my brain can tell it to be careful [characteristic of impulsivity associated with ADHD]."
- I have a certainty about the right way to play with the blocks [characteristic of some children with AS], and Jon was playing with them wrong and wouldn't stop playing wrong! So I had to stop him!"
- Carlos should know throwing away paper kills another tree, which causes species stress and global warming unnecessarily [characteristic of some children with gifted abilities to conceptualize global-environmental concerns]. I told him nicely in a quiet voice first!"

Young children usually are not introspective, insightful, or articulate enough to adequately explain their emotional and behavioral processes. As a result, their default answer, whether it is expressed or unexpressed, becomes "Because I'm a bad kid!" Adults "ask" rhetorical questions out of their own frustration. It serves everyone much better to say, "I don't like what you did." Or, "I'm angry about what you did." "Don't do that again." In other words, adults with high emotional intelligence who understand their own emotions are better able to present them in ways less likely to confuse children. Teachers with high emotional intelligence are better teachers!

4. *Managing Emotions.* Emotions convey information about experiences and processes to oneself if the emotions are not too painful to tolerate. Blocking out or minimizing overwhelming emotions may establish emotional comfort zones. Thus, individuals can monitor and regulate their and others' emotions to facilitate positive experiences and consequences. Adults and others may not be aware that children with challenges often exert exceptional energy trying to manage their emotions. In fact, such children almost always have to exert greater energy than other children in many areas of functioning. If fatigue, frustration, and repeated failures accumulate, unmanageable emotions eventually may explode. Managing emotions can become difficult for children with challenges who have depression or anxiety accumulated through numerous negative experiences. Children with AS, for example, may have potential neurological reasons as well that affect their ability to manage emotions (Attwood, 2006).

> There may be neurological reasons why there is a problem with emotion and management in general and anger management in particular. . . . In the case of people with Aspergers Syndrome . . . Information on the increasing emotional "heat" and functioning . . . (emotion and stress levels) are not available . . . as a warning of impending breakdown.
>
> This can explain why the child or adult does not appear to be consciously aware of increasing emotional stress, and his or her thoughts and behavior are not indicative of deterioration in mood. Eventually the degree of emotional stress is overwhelming, but it may be too late for the cognitive or thoughtful control of emotion. (p. 145)

Children with gifted abilities may have dysplasia, a disparity between a strong ability to cognitively understanding issues mismatched with a relatively limited ability to handle them emotionally. Gifted children don't always think, feel, or act as expected for their chronological ages. Morelock (1992) described ten-year-old Greg, who, when asked to write about a fight, wrote about more than two years of unhappy interactions with another boy. The other boy wrote only that they hit each other that day. Only the day's incident mattered to him. Greg held in years of frustration from various incidents that the other boy had forgotten almost as quickly as they happened. Children with special gifts or challenges or both may have different or more intense social-emotional realities. As a result, their relative emotional intelligence and other interpersonal skills become predictive of current and future social, academic, relationship, and vocational success or failures.

Overexcitability, which is a common trait among children with gifted abilities, can complicate management of emotions. Jackson and Peterson (2003) describe case studies of teenagers with gifted abilities who had "profound sensitivity" that contributed to deep feelings of depression. Many children with gifted abilities manage emotions through a great capacity to hide depression. They may have shame and a sense of failure from being unable to figure out causes and cures for their problems. Avoiding or hiding problems and suffering alone in silence, their problems often exacerbate, leading to further negative consequences. An exceptionally gifted teen compared his depression with his self-presentation:

> "I act like nothing's wrong. On some subconscious level it seems like some sort of weakness, some sort of vulnerability, and it hurts to share weaknesses. When you are gifted, you *feel* what other people feel; if someone else is depressed, you pick up on it, and it makes you feel depressed so you become afraid that your depression, when it happens, will evoke that feeling in someone else." (pp. 179–180)

Lovecky (2004) says girls with gifted abilities may actually hide their giftedness. Girls, who are often culturally trained to be socially mature and conscious, are more adaptive getting along and fitting in with peers. Fitting in at the cost of underperforming may be more compelling than opening, exploring, and revealing their gifted abilities. She says, "It is not uncommon to note that quite gifted girls mysteriously lose their abilities in average classrooms." She fears that "gifted, and especially those who are highly gifted, of minority groups, with ADHD, or any combination of these, may be even more at risk than are gifted boys" (p. 35). Their false presentation hides not only their gifts, but also any difficult underlying issues. Teachers need to actively foster an acceptance of excellence for girls in the classroom. Silverman (2005) of the Gifted Development Center believes that girls and women are underdiagnosed as gifted.

Many children with special needs do not have traits of resilience or social-emotional intelligence. The unluckiest ones do not have personal charisma or skills to enlist surrogate mentoring. Frustration, disappointment, social rejection, and adult impatience may cause them to develop highly negative personalities. Who needs great teachers and great parents? Not "cute" or resilient or emotionally intelligent children. They tend to do well anyway. They use their charm to get the adult support they need. Some children with challenges may not be able to manage emotions adequately to engage classmates or adults in positive reparative relationships. Instead, their actions repel caring adults. Well-intended adults, especially teachers, get punished for trying and eventually give up. As a result, children with challenges may lose potentially reparative relationships with teachers. Socially obnoxious kids need great mentors. Children who do not reward teachers for their effort and attention still need for them to hang in there with them. These are the children who desperately need the guidance and nurturing of adults that they cannot otherwise attract. They need very insightful and sophisticated teachers to see through and work through their off-putting negativity to reach the desperately lonely hearts within them.

Chapter Highlights

- The people of the real world may not have any desire, understanding, or compassion for individuals with challenges.

- For their emotional and psychological health, you need to disappoint children: specifically to stress them; allow frustration and failure; and let them suffer while experiencing stress, frustration, and failure!

- As with stress, frustration, and failure, only experience and practice with suffering develops emotional intelligence skills.

- Individuals with high emotional intelligence are less likely to engage in problem behaviors, and they avoid self-destructive, negative behaviors, or aggressive conflicts with others.

- Rejection and abandonment fears become prioritized emotions because of frequent victimization. Rather than facilitate thinking, emotions obscure thinking that could otherwise lead to functional choices for long-term success.

- Children with special gifts or challenges or both may have different or more intense social emotional realities.

- Socially obnoxious kids need great mentors. Children who do not reward teachers for their effort and attention still need for them to hang in there with them.

3

Creating Powerful and Successful Children

WIN SO HE WOULD THROW A TANTRUM

"Noooo! You cheated! You dirty cheater! You stupid . . . Leave me alone! Stupid game . . . you cheated!" Sound familiar? Ten-year-old Harvey threw tremendous tantrums when he lost. He cried, screamed, accused others of cheating, threw the game, stomped out, and sulked. Family and classmates didn't want to play with him. The issue was not that he had to win, but that he hated to lose . . . couldn't lose. Losing or not being "right" somehow had come to mean to him that he was unworthy. When children feel that they "gotta win," it creates two significant risky strategies: First, the only option to guarantee that they will never lose or fail would be to not try anymore. Avoidance of any risk becomes their life strategy, which means losing opportunities for growth. Second, children would be willing to do anything in order to win. Winning at any cost opens up a whole slew of potentially toxic behaviors. In the extreme, that may mean developing conduct disorder (American Psychiatric Association, 1994, p. 85). In adulthood, individuals may develop socio-pathic values. When winning at any cost becomes paramount, other values such as fairness, integrity, honesty, and respect become irrelevant and are seen as obstacles to winning. Harvey was gifted. He began reading early, was adept athletically, and had insight and complex perspectives that astonished and charmed adults. Since things came easily, he became used to mastering things without working hard. Subsequently, if something could not be easily mastered, his self-esteem suffered. He would try to avoid it. If he had to try anyway, he would get over-whelmed or throw tantrums. Harvey lacked a key component to be truly successful.

Harvey had intellect and passion, but did not have the zeal or affirmative drive to overcome obstacles. While some children redouble their efforts when confronted with obstacles, others are thwarted by challenges. Despite strengths or gifted abilities, such children are not destined to become successful adults. Striving to deal with any "hindrances" that arise in their paths is essential for achievement. Author Macolm Gladwell (Wargo, 2006) was the number one-rated Canadian runner at age thirteen to fourteen. However, early precocity did not translate into being a champion runner later. He suffered disappointments and setbacks and gave up running for several years. He did not have the drive necessary to persevere to overcome his obstacles. Of fifteen nationally ranked runners of that age group, only one eventually became a top runner in his prime at age twenty-four. He had been "gawky" and one of the poorer runners when younger. Gladwell felt that the runner had succeeded largely because, like Mozart, he "practiced, practiced, practiced." Beyond innate ability, success comes from working hard and circumstances that promote hard work, such as adult direction, support, and guidance.

Teachers of young children instinctively try to promote these attributes by prompting children to keep trying and to try harder. Teachers realize that children's continued efforts are essential to their eventual success. Teachers emphasize, praise, and reward effort from preschool throughout elementary school. "You tried so hard. Good for you!" A C for performance with an A for effort gets children a B grade. As teachers reward children's effort, care needs to be taken that feigned effort without performance is not rewarded. "But I tried!" may be about children who have learned to manipulate teacher support of effort, rather than their actual effort. Determined effort needs to result sooner or later in higher performance and the subsequent rewards. Harvey's balance between effort and performance had become convoluted. He had not developed the determination to make the sustained effort that normally results in greater performance or successes. For most people, success becomes rewarding, which makes expending the effort rewarding as well. Harvey became determined not to gain the rewards per se, but not to fail. He might feign effort or claim to exert great effort, but expending great effort could not be rewarding without success. In fact, expending great effort and not winning was an ultimate blow to his self-esteem. So he minimized his effort in order to avoid risking such a blow, putting him at greater risk of failure, causing more self-esteem deterioration. Harvey's negative cycle intensified, deepening his frustration.

Other therapists, but not teachers, sometimes are surprised to learn that when playing games with children, I often beat them. Many adults assume children are too fragile to suffer losing. Quite the contrary, "throwing" games to children implies to them that they are too fragile and not powerful enough to handle disappointment, frustration, or failure. It is critical to give children the opportunity to suffer failure within a healthy framework. No one is better able to help children deal with losing than caring adults, who best understand their capacities and challenges. Intimidated or put off by Harvey's potential tantrums, classmates avoided playing with him. Adults, if unable to avoid playing games with him, purposely lost to him. Sensitive to his issues, I would win so he would be provoked into a tantrum! Instead of taunting him and then leaving him furious and alone, as classmates would do, I engaged him about it. I then supported him by calmly validating how badly he felt. I validated his core worth whether or not he won. With training, his parents and his teacher duplicated this process when they played with him. They also facilitated his play with other children at home and in the classroom and playground. They set clear boundaries and expectations if Harvey wanted to play and monitored him carefully. As a result, they were prepared to give him immediate guidance, including removing him from the game or play if he began to throw a tantrum. They kept reminding him to use his intellect to consider his logical choices versus illogical choices. Eventually, with growth and practice, he could keep playing and consider values such as honesty, fair play, cooperation, empathy, and compassion. He became more fun to play with. Harvey stopped being so obnoxious and his social interactions with classmates improved.

THE NEXT *SS* IS FOR *SENSITIVITY* AND *SUPPORT*

Children light up with joy with a smile from a parent, a "way to go!" from a teacher, or a frantic greeting from the puppy dog. Aren't you pleased when someone remembers your name or your hobby or favorite sports team? You and your preferences were important enough to be remembered! When your baby said "Mama," or "Dada," didn't your heart fill with joy? Verbal affirmations or nurturing along with other actions are necessary to support children. The earlier directives to stress 'em, frustrate 'em, make sure they fail and suffer too, without qualification sound neglectful or abusive. Adults need to monitor and regulate the process with sensitivity to children's individual challenges, needs, and strengths. Sensitivity must define support. Children with challenges have uniqueness with special qualities and needs. These qualities and needs often require specific support. Sensitivity to Harvey, who had gifted abilities and could not stand to lose, directed adult support to require him losing games. Sensitivity directed support consisting of emotionally nurturing him with clarifying messages regarding his inherent self-worth. Sensitivity to children with nonverbal learning disabilities, who may feel stress but have difficulty connecting it to words (Whitney, 2002, p. 35), should prompt adult support to help them anticipate and articulate feelings in language they can understand and eventually use themselves. If children have issues with impulsivity and hyperactivity, supportive adults identify potentially challenging situations in advance. Then they can offer clear and firm boundaries before problematic behavior develops. Sensitive adults reframe academic and social challenges for children with AS so that challenged self-esteem can be regained through guided problem solving. In general, adults can anticipate likely stumbling blocks and triggers based on awareness of individual children's traits and history academically, socially, and behaviorally. Thus prepared, adults can institute preventative measures and offer guidance and boundaries to preclude more intense problems.

Children are not well served with generic or projected adult sensitivity. Generic sensitivity assumes that other children's experiences are applicable to a specific child. For example, assumptions that children are often anxious about new experiences could prompt generic support inappropriate for children who may welcome new challenges. Another assumption may be that a child with LD or ADHD has low self-esteem. High self-esteem may be the greatest strength of a particular child, so that praise would not be as supportive as teaching specific compensations. Projected sensitivity occurs when adults anxiously project their personal issues as applicable to children. For example, if adults felt they were rejected when disciplined in their childhood, they assume that children will feel rejected when disciplined. As a result, they may hesitate or refrain unnecessarily from applying appropriate consequences when children misbehave. With all the demands of managing a classroom of children, personal growth for teachers to address these issues becomes critical. Such growth leads to better abilities to distinguish between children's needs and adult anxiety and to avoid unnecessary support that can be intrusive. No matter how well intended, unnecessary support can breed resentment or, worse, teach vulnerability. Children may conclude adults don't really understand them. Teacher awareness of each child's individuality enables teachers to offer the specific support that each child needs.

THE NEXT *SS* IS FOR *SKILLS* AND *STRENGTH*

When supported with sensitivity, children develop skills and strength from facing challenges. Emotional, mental, and spiritual strengths come from personal struggle and are required to manage emotions. Strength is not only taking on and surmounting arduous tasks, but also bouncing back from frustration and failure. Problem solving involves developing specific skills through experiences from success and failure. Skills and strength positively reciprocate to further increase skills and strength. The more skillfully individuals address challenges, the more strength improves. And greater strength with subsequent confidence and resiliency facilitates skills. Specific skills are required to compensate for specific learning disabilities. For example, using mnemonics, making word associations, and writing lists are skills that help compensate for short-term memory issues. Teachers can guide children with ADHD to develop skills addressing their impulsivity, hyperactivity, and distractibility. "Stop and think" strategies create the possibility of better decision-making skills. Sitting in the front of the room helps with distractibility since it narrows the child's field of vision. That removes multiple classmates out of their visual horizon to their side and behind them. Developing note-taking skills, especially in choosing the most important element to write down, helps children with distraction issues or auditory processing issues focus and pay attention. Such effective skills may be developed instinctively or overtly taught by teachers or other adults. Sometimes, other instinctively developed "skills" can be very helpful . . . or not.

Shay paid attention but couldn't sit still. He had trouble maintaining eye contact and was often drawn to examine his visually stimulating classroom. When the teacher scolded him for not paying attention, he would honestly retort that he was paying attention. She would be annoyed at his denial, and their negative cycle of accusation and denial would ensue. When Shay told me that he paid attention in class, he was looking for little Waldos in the *Where's Waldo* (Handford, 1987) book. Without missing a beat in our conversation, he found little Waldos hidden in successive two-page layouts without ever giving me eye contact. All the time he was bouncing in his seat. He was paying attention! He actually had a skill of paying attention auditorially, integrating information, formulating and expressing appropriate responses without using eye contact. The teacher didn't realize or believe his fidgeting and wandering eye contact could coexist with attention. Feeling unappreciated for this "skill" or strength, he felt unjustly accused by the teacher. Aware of his outrage, I offered to teach him another "skill." I suggested teaching him to "fool" the teacher into thinking that he was paying attention even though he already was paying attention! After a hilarious negotiation, Shay agreed that it would be fun to fool the teacher. I taught him the "skill" of fidgeting, shaking legs, waving fingers, and eyes wandering, but only when the teacher was writing on the board or otherwise facing away from him. Then I showed him how to gaze intently at her when she looked in his direction. Occasionally, he was to nod his head, tilt it, widen his eyes, and purse his lips to indicate interest, attention, or concentration. I explained that his teacher would interpret these cues to mean that he was paying attention. Two weeks later with a big smile, he told how the teacher now "thinks I'm paying attention!" although he always had been. Shay actually had learned how to be attentive to others. He had learned how to adapt for his social presentation to others. As a result, Shay was able to make behavioral compensations for some of his ADHD issues. Sensitive to his outrage from the injustice of false accusations, I had activated his strengths (sense of humor and irony, role playing, etc.). I had taught him this "skill" playfully and sarcastically. He felt better understood and became receptive to other suggestions to facilitate skills development and improving emotional intelligence. Who "fooled" whom?

AS may cause problems interpreting the meaning of a verbal communication, including identifying the key element in a communication. Individuals with this problem often pick out a minor or almost irrelevant element in a communication on which to focus or respond. They miss what the speaker intends them to recognize as the most important issue. This problem is also indicative of a poorly functioning theory of mind. The theory of mind is "the way somebody conceives of mental activity in others, including how children conceptualize mental activity in others and how they attribute intention to and predict the behavior of others" (MSN Encarta Dictionary, 2008). For example, if a teacher says, "You took the teacher's sharp scissors to cut your project. They aren't for children," this statement has

- an implicit meaning constituting a directive for the child to give back the scissors; the child should respond to the directive;
- a warning that sharp scissors are dangerous for children to handle in general; and
- a specific injunction for the child not to handle the scissors since they are dangerous for the child to handle (since the child qualifies under the general category of "children").

However, due to confusion determining the key elements of communications from a poor theory of mind, the child may focus on other elements and respond in any of the following ways:

- "I didn't take the scissors to cut my project. I took it to cut a loose thread." [a mistaken focus on why the child took the scissors]
- "I didn't take the scissors. Billy gave it to me." [a mistaken focus on how the child got the scissors]
- "Scissors aren't that sharp. Razors are sharp. My dad has a sharp razor I can't touch." [a mistaken focus on the relative sharpness of scissors]

- "My mom has scissors like that, she calls them sewing scissors. What are teacher's scissors?" [a mistaken focus on the labeling of types of scissors]
- "I use scissors just like that at home. How come I can't use them at school?" [a mistaken focus on whether the scissors are for children or not]

Adults may think children who respond this way are being purposely obstinate or sarcastic. Most children develop the skill of identifying the key element through their observation of others. It is not usually overtly taught because adults assume children have already naturally acquired the skill. John Elder Robison (2007), in his autobiography, *Look Me in the Eyes,* describes his many problems from not having this skill. People did not realize his difficulty picking out what was most important to them amidst the words they spoke. He often responded incorrectly because of focusing on what he mistook to be the intention of the communication. Others assumed that he didn't care, was being disrespectful, weird, or purposely difficult. When he was young, adults did not know that he needed to be overtly taught this skill. It was the diagnosis of AS well into adulthood that led to him working on this challenge. Through trial and error, he eventually learned to recognize the key elements in communication more adroitly.

Children with gifted abilities may set their standards high. They may expect themselves to do and be more than their abilities allow. Adults need to be sensitive to the potential turmoil they may suffer from the discrepancy between desires and performance. Children with gifted abilities in turmoil may not develop the emotional and psychological skills to prevent self-esteem loss. They often feel that they should be able to not only consistently perform superbly, but also be able to handle the frustration of failing to consistently perform superbly. In other words, to be perfect! Ironically, skills or strengths may create deficits in other areas. This may come from some children's resistance to seeking help to develop their lesser skills. It is natural for individuals to gravitate to areas or activities of skill and strength that reward them with multiple rewards and success. It is equally natural to avoid areas or activities that are not rewarding or where one is hard put to be successful. As a result, relatively minor challenges can become significant weaknesses when they are consistently avoided. Avoidance of stress, frustration, failure, and suffering prevents compensating for challenges. When individuals consistently work on their challenges, the result is often that they develop tremendous compensating strengths. On the other hand, adults need to be aware that any strength also has the potential to become a weakness. An examination of the four major challenges focused on in this book finds each of them consisting of major strengths in the appropriate contexts. The consideration of these issues as challenges or weaknesses derives largely from the demands of the academic and social context of the classroom. Later, the demands of many vocational situations may accentuate the challenges negatively. The modern classroom often demands aptitudes and behaviors that are difficult for some children. In other times and circumstances, these children may have found avenues and vocations that exploited their strengths and minimized their challenges. Children need teachers to balance the misfit between explicit and implicit demands for classroom behavior and children's natural abilities. Without appropriate support and guidance, this misfit can activate children's challenges and turn them into enduring weaknesses.

SF IS FOR *SURVIVE* AND *FLOURISH*

Adults often try to reassure children who are struggling by saying, "You're OK." That may be one of the worse things an adult can say to children in the midst of a distressful episode. That comment completely disregards their reality in the moment. In the moment, they are definitely *not* OK! They should retort, "Do I look OK with the tears running down my face? Do I sound OK?" Encouragement is great, but denying children's reality is not. However, the slightly different statement, "You will be OK," affirms to them that they will at least survive and offers them the possibility that they will also flourish. Adult confidence helps both adults and children address what it takes to survive. Once negative feelings and experiences are addressed skillfully and strength increases, children realize they can endure failure. They realize they will survive preschool or kindergarten, phonics or math facts, P.E. or choir, loss of friends or the new school, the mean kid or being alone. Letting Harvey lose games showed him that he could tolerate the disappointment, still be OK, and survive. Shay learned that he could struggle with a teacher and develop skills and strength to persevere. John Elder Robison found that his AS did not stop him from continuing in life and relationships. Knowing that one will at least survive facilitates a sense of purpose and belief in a bright future, goal directedness, motivation, and aspirations. These are all characteristics of resilient children (Risk, protection, and resilience, 2001).

Arnold et al. (2005, p. 205) say research finds a raised percentage of depression in children with LD. The survey of literature conducted by Spencer, Wilens, Biederman, Wozniak, and Harding-Crawford (2000) finds a significant comorbidity between ADHD and mood disorders. Brasic (2006) states, "Depression and hypomania are common among adolescents and adults with Asperger disorder, particularly those with a family history of these conditions. An increased risk of suicide exists, with risks possibly rising in proportion to the number and severity of comorbid maladies" (p. 8). The most salient characteristics of adolescents with gifted abilities may be associated with vulnerability to social and emotional disturbances: (a) perfectionism, (b) supersensitivy, (c) social isolation, and (d) sensory overexcitability (De Souza Fleith, 2001). Skills and strength fostered by adult sensitivity and support help children retain a sense of hope and of future rewards. When hope evolves into faith in survival, then children can develop the ability to risk emotional, psychological, intellectual, spiritual, and physical investment to try to flourish. Not all survivors flourish, but those that do may accomplish wonderful things. LD, ADHD, AS, or giftedness have motivated many individuals, famous and unknown, historical and contemporary people, to develop great skills and strength and to subsequently survive and flourish. An Internet search with the words "famous people" and "learning disabilities," finds many examples:

> Like many people with a handicap, I compensated elsewhere. When I had difficulty with spelling and reading, I concentrated on mathematics and sports. However back in class, I found traditional teaching methods such as standing up and reading aloud in class pure torture. Dyslexia gave me a different way of looking at things. A compulsion to dissect ideas and concepts from every possible angle has stayed with me.
>
> —Marco Pierre White, chef and restaurateur (*Famous people with dyslexia*, n.d., Artists & designers section, ¶ 16)

> *Grey's Anatomy* star Patrick Dempsey says his childhood wasn't so McDreamy: He wasn't diagnosed as being dyslexic until he was 12 years old. "I think it's made me who I am today," says Dempsey, who plays neurosurgeon Dr. Derek Shepherd on the hit ABC series, in an interview on *The Barbara Walters Special* . . ."It's given me a perspective of—you have to keep working," Dempsey tells Walters. "I have never given up." Dempsey, 40, says he struggles while reading scripts and memorizing his lines.
>
> —*Grey's Anatomy*'s Dempsey has dyslexia, 2006.

> I have learned how to be different. After I learned to be different, I enjoyed being different. It is so much fun to walk to a different drummer.
>
> —Delos R. Smith, global economist (*Famous people with dyslexia*, n.d., Entrepreneurs section, ¶ 23)

> I never read in school. . . . In the second week of the 11th grade, I just quit. . . . Almost everything I learned, I had to learn by listening.

My report cards always said that I was not living up to my potential. Don't focus on how dyslexia makes life tougher ... instead ... hear the invisible voices of creativity that sing louder in your heart that those less fortunate people who have not been given our gift (curse) to challenge them to greater heights. Make peace with it and fly!

—Cher, singer and actress (*Famous dyslexics*, n.d. ¶ 14;
Famous people with dyslexia, n.d., Musicians & Vocalists section, ¶ 3)

I had to train myself to focus my attention. I became very visual and learned how to create mental images in order to comprehend what I read.

—Tom Cruise, actor (*Famous people with dyslexia*, n.d.,
Movie industry section, ¶ 13)

Michael Phelps, winner of a record eight gold medals in the 2008 Summer Olympics in Beijing, China, and his mother, Debbie, told host Bob Costas of NBC Sports that he was diagnosed with ADHD as a child. They discovered that his energy along with physical gifts made him a "genius" as a swimmer. His gifted athletic abilities as a swimmer won him early successes in age-group swim meets, but also targeted him for bullying by certain other swimmers. Phelps spoke of how that and other negative experiences motivated him to work hard to succeed and of the support that his mother and coaches gave him all along the way (Costas, 2008). Stress 'em, frustrate 'em, let them experience failure and suffering so they can struggle! Support with sensitivity so that skills and strength will develop. Sensitivity is impossible without understanding both children and the specific challenges they have. Skills and strength are required to meet those challenges and to acquire confidence that they can survive and can hope and invest in flourishing. That is how teachers and other adults create powerful and successful children

- who have emotional intelligence;
- who have resiliency;
- who understand and compensate successfully for their challenges;
- who accept themselves with high self-esteem;
- who are healthy, responsible, and responsive members of classrooms, families, and communities;
- who are too skilled and strong to be successfully victimized; and
- who are too competent and confident in themselves to need to become bullies.

The following is a summary of the principles of *SFFS SS SS SF* to create a powerful and successful child.

SFFS SS SS SF

Principles for Becoming Powerful and Successful, or How to Build a Powerful and Successful Child

Stress

One must experience stress, since stress is what builds strength. Avoiding stress avoids opportunities to grow.

Frustrate

One must experience frustration to learn how to survive it and deal with it successfully, since it accompanies life experiences, stresses, and challenges. Avoiding frustration results in avoiding the stress that builds.

Fail

One must experience and become comfortable with failure, since failure is a natural consequence of trying anything or learning anything. Fear of failure results in one of two consequences: one will become sociopathic and willing to win at all costs, no matter how harmful it is to oneself, others, or the community; or, to guarantee no failure, one will not try.

Suffer

While experiencing stress, frustration, and failure, one must also suffer in order to experience that one can suffer without being destroyed or overwhelmed and to discover one's resiliency. If a person feels unable to tolerate any suffering, then that person will do extreme compulsive behaviors in order to avoid suffering.

Sensitivity

A person can endure stress, frustration, failure, and suffering if caring authoritative individuals have the sensitivity to understand the person's abilities, limitations, and capacities.

Support

With that sensitivity, then such caring authoritative individuals can offer the appropriate support that one needs to benefit from stress, frustration, failure, and suffering.

Strength

From the experiences with sensitive support, one will develop strength.

Skills

From the experiences with sensitive support, one will develop skills.

Survive

From the experiences, strength, and skills, one will develop a confidence that, despite the difficulties and challenges of the world, one will survive.

Flourish

Once a person is confident of survival, then that person can risk and have the opportunity to flourish in the world.

All individuals must go through stress, frustration, failure, and suffering to grow powerful. To build powerful successful children, adults must stress, frustrate, let their children fail, and make sure they suffer! With sensitivity, they can support children through this to develop strength and skills that will ensure survival and offer the possibility and opportunity of flourishing.

Chapter Highlights

- When winning at any cost becomes paramount, other values such as fairness, integrity, honesty, and respect become irrelevant and are seen as obstacles to winning.

- Teachers realize that children's continued effort is essential to their eventual success.

- The demands for performance become increasingly pronounced as children progress through school and begin to enter the real world.

- No one is better able to help children deal with losing than caring adults, who best understand their capacities and challenges.

- Adults need to monitor and regulate the process with sensitivity to children's individual challenges, needs, and strengths. Sensitivity must define support.

- The more skillfully individuals address challenges, the more strength improves. And greater strength with subsequent confidence and resiliency facilitates skills.

- It is natural for individuals to gravitate to areas or activities of skill and strength that reward them with multiple rewards and success. It is equally natural to avoid areas or activities that are not rewarding or where one is hard put to be successful.

- When hope evolves into faith in survival, then children can develop the ability to risk emotional, psychological, intellectual, spiritual, and physical investment to try to flourish.

4

Social Cues

WHO IS THIS KID?

Jerry was about to go to kindergarten. At least that's what his parents thought. He had a lot of odd behaviors unlike other five-year-olds. He would startle easily as if some monster snatched him unexpectedly from his own little world. He frequently seemed mystified about what other kids wanted—an ineffective theory of mind. He could not anticipate how others would respond to common situations or to him. He was usually anxious without apparent reason. His spoken language—volume, intonation, inflection, and rate of speech—were off. Other children noticed . . . something. Jerry did not play well with them. He got mad when they weren't playing with toys "the right way." He grabbed toys from others. He sometimes unexpectedly hit them without provocation. They got disturbed when he got upset, began screaming, or became inconsolable over seemingly trivial things. A couple of children with their own emotional and behavioral issues got into frequent conflicts with him. More vigilant supervision became necessary to prevent children from picking on him. Something was off. I met and gave the parents a list of Jerry's behaviors. This was the list:

1. Startles unexpectedly

2. Doesn't understand what other kids want

3. Anxious for no apparent reasons

4. Confused

5. Often speaks without inflection

6. Avoids spontaneous social interactions

7. Trouble sustaining a conversation

8. Suddenly hits or pushes without apparent provocation

9. Plays with toys over and over (ritualistic?)

10. Cries inconsolably over small issues

11. Frequent toileting accidents

12. Problems with transitions

13. Trouble making friends

14. Often clingy with adults

15. Takes disposed food from garbage cans to eat

What had they observed at home? Although they were vague, it seemed that the behaviors were familiar to them. I got permission for a special education teacher to informally observe and give feedback. Without venturing a specific diagnosis, she agreed that Jerry needed further professional evaluation from specialists. Jerry's parents said they would look into it. However, they felt that Jerry would "grow out of it." I responded that I was professionally compelled to assert that his behavior was not strictly developmental and would not change with maturity. Parents need teachers to give them the benefits of the knowledge gained from their professional work, whether parents want the information or not! (For a more extensive step-by-step discussion on how to present information to parents who may not want to hear it, you can refer to pages 137–144 of my book, *Difficult Behavior in Early Childhood: Positive Discipline for PreK–3 Classrooms and Beyond*.) We felt that Jerry's behaviors were probably indicative of other issues. Over the next several weeks, I asked them if they had sought out any resources or help. They never did. Eventually, they withdrew Jerry from my school. How many times has something like that happened to teachers who confront parents with challenging feedback? Many parents are disturbed but grateful to get honest feedback from teachers. Sometimes, teacher feedback confirms a concern that they already have noticed. Unfortunately, because it can be difficult to consider that their child has a serious issue, avoidance and denial may be parental responses when teachers bring up potentially sensational issues. Schwartz-Watts (2005) examined early attempts at intervention with a five-year old who was diagnosed with pervasive developmental disorder. "Each time the defendant attended a new school his teachers became aware of his impaired functioning and sent him for evaluation. His parents did not follow up with any treatments, although they were recommended" (p. 390). Further review of records and interviews confirmed an autistic spectrum disorder that the court and the authors felt contributed to emotional and psychological damage over many years.

Jerry was showing behavioral issues at five years old that predicted more serious issues to come. Jerry's parents eventually were able to accept that something was not working for him, but not for several years.

Asperger Syndrome—Rote Learning

Not six days, six weeks, or six months, but six *years* later, Jerry's mother called. Jerry's current school district had just diagnosed Jerry as having some autistic issue. She wanted me, the first person to bring up a concern, to report my observations from six years before. Although somewhat gratified to be finally heard and confirmed, I was furious it had taken six years of failure and frustration. There must have been so many lost opportunities for intervention. Significant damage to Jerry's self-esteem must have occurred before the diagnosis was finally explored and confirmed and intervention initiated. In addition, I should have been the fourth professional, not the first, to bring up something of concern to them. Before he ever came to my program, other professionals met and knew Jerry. He had an infant/toddler caregiver, another preschool teacher, and, of course, a pediatrician. They hadn't intervened with feedback about Jerry's easily observable and out-of-the-norm behavior. Pediatricians in particular are the historical "go-to" professionals when parents have concerns about developmental progression and norms. While they may be experts in physical development and medical issues, some pediatricians have minimal training and knowledge about child emotional, psychological, social, and cognitive development. Parents often go to them to seek their advice or opinions about the information conveyed to them by the professionals with the most experience with child development: early childhood educators such as daycare, preschool, kindergarten, and early elementary school teachers. Some pediatricians incorrectly tell parents, "Your child is fine," when a teacher's education, experience, and expertise says something is not fine. Aaaargh! Both children and parents depend on teachers to assert their extensive education, experience, and expertise about child development. Finally, after six years, enough professionals in Jerry's life gave honest feedback and his parents sought help.

Jerry had AS or some other form of high-functioning autism. Issues on the autism spectrum, including pervasive developmental disorder, are commonly addressed through intensive training, often utilizing rote learning. Expecting children like Jerry to perceive, interpret, integrate, and respond in social situations when compromised by AS creates frustration for everyone.

Children develop relationships primarily through the interactive process of play, including being playful. Being playful invites reciprocity. With greater verbal skills, conversation becomes critical to play. AS fundamentally affects communication, play, and relationships. Bauer (1996) notes that

> Pragmatic, or conversational, language skills often are weak because of problems with turn-taking, a tendency to revert to areas of special interest or difficulty sustaining the "give and take" of conversations. Many children with AS have difficulties dealing with humor, tending not to "get" jokes or laughing at the wrong time; this is in spite of the fact that quite a few show an interest in humor and jokes, particularly things such as puns or word games. The common belief that children with pervasive developmental disorders are humorless is frequently mistaken. Some children with AS tend to be hyperverbal, not understanding that this interferes with their interactions with others and puts others off. (Clinical Features section, ¶ 3)

My middle-school clients with AS often got into verbal sparring bouts with others—and me! They try to make sure they "win" or prove themselves right and the other person wrong.

Jerry's social problems caused him to be readily identified by aggressive children for teasing or bullying. *Your Little Professor,* an online resource, discusses the targeting of children with AS (referred to as "Aspies") for bullying:

> The reason is that Aspies fit the profile of a typical victim: a "loner" who appears different from other children. Like hungry wolves that attack a limping sheep that can't keep up with the herd, the Aspie with his clumsy body language and poor social skills appears vulnerable and ripe for bullying. . . .
>
> Luke Jackson, a thirteen-year-old boy with Asperger Syndrome writing in his book *Freaks, Geeks & Asperger Syndrome,* explains it like this:
>
> "AS kids don't realize which things they are supposed to go home and tell. 'What have you done at school today?' wouldn't automatically bring about the answer 'I have been bullied' unless that subject was specifically brought up.
>
> " . . . But no amount of threatening by my brother, by the teachers, fear of expulsion, pleasant reasoning, absolutely nothing made any difference and [bullies] never left me alone. In the end they were physically pushing me around and punching me and it was about the worst time of my entire life."

One principal told a parent of an Aspie, "Your son is a little different and it bothers other children, so he brings this on himself because of who he is." Also in such a school, teachers and coaches bully the child too. (*Bullying [and Asperger syndrome]*, ¶ 4–9)

The comment that "he brings this on himself" fundamentally betrays children who depend on teachers and other educators to manage the social dynamics in the school community. No child ever asks to be bullied. It is true that some children are more vulnerable to become victimized, but that should never be justification for it happening. With such children, adults in roles of authority have a greater responsibility to facilitate appropriate interactions.

Social Cues

Characteristic of AS, Jerry missed social cues, especially nonverbal social cues, that are extremely critical to interpersonal communication. Facial cues include muscle tension or relaxation around the eyes and mouth, and tilting, leaning, or nodding one's head. Additional communication comes from combinations of changes in breathing and expansive to very slight movements of the hands, arms, body, and legs.

Nonverbal communication is quite possibly the most important part of the communicative process, for researchers now know that our actual words carry far less meaning than nonverbal cues. For example, repeat many times the following sentence, emphasizing different words in the sentence each time you do so: "I beat my spouse last night." Does not the meaning of the sentence change? The words themselves carry many meanings, depending upon nonverbal cues, in the case, inflection. Essentially, the study of nonverbal communication is broken down to:

- environmental clues
- spatial study
- physical appearance
- behavioral cues
- vocal qualities
- body motion or kinesics." (Long Beach City College Foundation, 2004, p. 100)

Successful expressive communication and receptive communication are the keys to intimacy, trust, and relationships. They draw support, compliance, or allegiance critical from potential peers. These are all keys to social survival and potentially academic and vocational survival. In "Body Language in Debating," Mandic (2008) promotes ten compelling nonverbal forms of communication applicable to day-to-day communications.

1. *Vocal.* We respond to the dynamic, rhythmic, melodic and accent, stress, or tempo components of someone's voice. Silence can be a very powerful message, as can raising or lowering the voice. . . .

2. *Facial.* The face is the most expressive part of our body. Macro and micro facial expressions are strong messages usually connected to feelings, attitudes and personal belief systems. . . .

3. *Gestural.* Gestural aspects of body language . . . are understood in connection to contexts and relationships with other people. . . .

4. *Postural.* The postural aspect of someone's communication relates to the position of the body in a dialoguing context. The whole body is a unit of communication. . . .

5. *Proxemic.* The proxemic aspect includes communication through physical contact [including both touching oneself or others]. . . .

6. *Spatial.* The spatial aspect [uses space to communicate issues such as] dominance, acceptance, extroversion, [or] respect. . . .

7. *Rhythm.* The rhythm of breathing, eye movement, hands and legs, and the whole body gives meaning to someone's expression. . . . Sudden changes in rhythm will increase attention and stress the importance of the speaker's point.

8. *Movement.* Movement is a macro statement in communication . . . [and] can reveal basic motives, character traits and some practical intents of the person moving.

9. *Clothing and Body Decoration.* These aspects are dependent on individual and cultural standards or ideals. . . .

10. *Drawing.* Drawing is a natural . . . form of communication [that may be especially relevant with younger children who are preverbal or have difficulty verbally articulating]. (¶ 5–15)

Nonverbal sensitivity, awareness, freedom and creativity have enormous impact. Becoming nonverbally fluent, centered, grounded, and flexible not only develops self-esteem, fluency, and flexibility, but also enables better communication skills and relationships in life. Gordon and Fleisher (2002, p. 84) described how interviewers determine an interviewee's truthfulness by observing a multitude of nonverbal cues. The principles and assumptions they discuss mirror processes people intuitively use to determine the honesty or deceptiveness of others' communication.

Nonverbal behavior:	
Indicative of Truth	Indicative of Deception
Genuinely friendly	Overly friendly
Direct answers	Evasive answers
Good eye contact	Poor eye contact
Cooperative	Uncooperative
Lighthearted	Scared
Composed	Nervous facial movement
Relaxed	Nervous bodily movement
Talkative	Not talkative
Overall truthful appearance	Overall deceptive appearance

Nonverbal differences:	
Truthful Suspect	Deceptive Suspect
Relaxed and confident	Tense and defensive
Face-to-face body alignment	Evasive body alignment
Increased use of illustrators	Use of adaptors
Natural and settled foot and body positions	Tense repetitive, restless foot and body movements

Children who have trouble interpreting social cues may also not present social cues in the same manner as others. Children with challenges may inadvertently present nonverbal cues that others assume to be deceptive and harboring harmful or negative intent. Several deceptive characteristics such as "tense and defensive," being "scared," or "nervous facial or body movement" could be their reactions to frequent teasing or frustration or failure socially and academically. Other characteristics considered deceptive may actually be characteristics of a particular challenge. For example, unusual body alignment or a slight physical awkwardness of some children with AS might be considered "evasive body alignment." Other characteristic behaviors such as repetitive rocking or self-soothing physical tics and difficulty maintaining eye contact may be interpreted as deceptive and "tense repetitive, restless foot and body movements" and "poor eye contact." "Evasive answers" may come from gifted children responding to nuances or fascinating alternative perspectives unanticipated by a listener. A response may be considered "uncooperative" when ADHD distractibility and impulsivity draws both attention and behavior to other urgencies. It is therefore not surprising that people may interpret the nonverbal social cues of children with special needs as aloof, defiant, or disrespectful. Adults can only accurately recognize negative nonverbal social cues from common nonverbal expressions of specific challenges if they understand children's individuality.

REASONS INDIVIDUALS DON'T GET IT!

LD, ADHD, AS, and giftedness have been referenced regarding misinterpretation of nonverbal social cues. Placing these challenges among other issues affecting social cues recognition can lead to teachers differentiating interventions for supporting children. Jerry's issue, AS, is one of at least eleven reasons for missing social cues.

1. Asperger syndrome

2. Physical disability

3. Cross-cultural issues

4. Overstimulation

5. Denial

6. Anxiety

7. Neurosis

8. Disassociation

9. Learning disabilities

10. Attention deficit disorder (or attention deficit hyperactivity disorder)

11. Intoxication/substance abuse

Figure 4.1 lists these reasons along with accompanying intervention strategies. The following chapter has descriptions of the next ten reasons for missing social cues in addition to AS. Many reasons have significant cross-relevance to the other processing or learning issues. Each of the four major challenges discussed in this book potentially not only causes problems reading social cues, but can also stigmatize individuals and increase vulnerability to low self-esteem and bullying. Recognizing and distinguishing each issue also leads to a matching response or intervention to help individuals better recognize social cues.

Figure 4.1

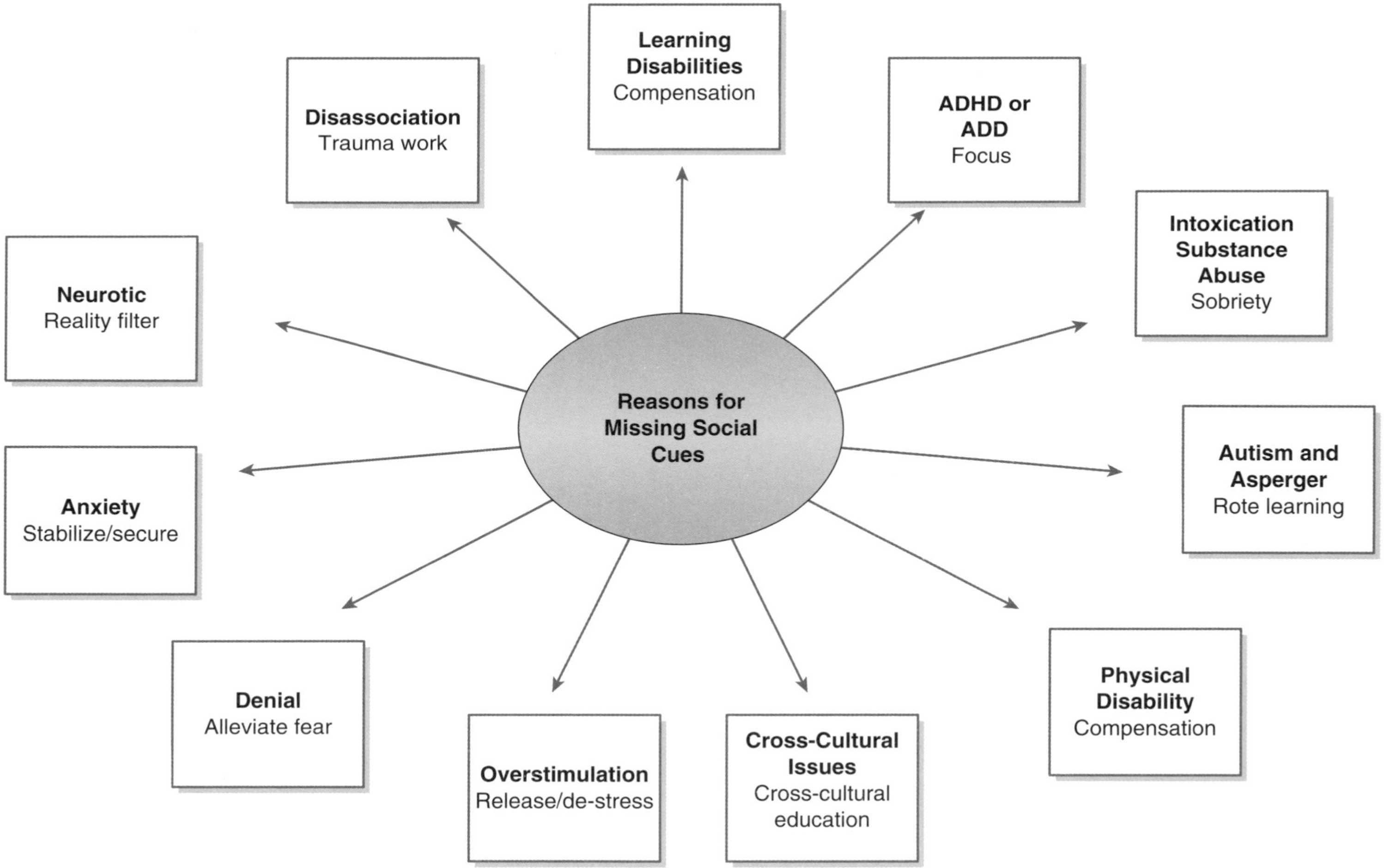

Reasons for Missing Social Cues

Intoxication Substance Abuse — Sobriety

Autism and Asperger — Rote learning

Physical Disability — Compensation

ADHD or ADD — Focus

Cross-Cultural Issues — Cross-cultural education

Learning Disabilities — Compensation

Overstimulation — Release/de-stress

Disassociation — Trauma work

Denial — Alleviate fear

Neurotic — Reality filter

Anxiety — Stabilize/secure

Chapter Highlights

- Because it can be difficult to consider that their children may have a serious issue, avoidance and denial may be parental responses when teachers bring up potentially sensational issues.

- Both children and parents depend on teachers to assert their extensive education, experience, and expertise about child development.

- Children develop relationships primarily through the interactive process of play, including being playful. Being playful invites reciprocity. With greater verbal skills, conversation becomes critical to play.

- Social cues, especially nonverbal social cues, are extremely critical to interpersonal communication. Facial cues include muscle tension or relaxation around the eyes and mouth, and tilting, leaning, or nodding one's head.

- Becoming nonverbally fluent, centered, grounded, and flexible not only develops self-esteem, fluency, and flexibility, but also enables better communication skills and relationships in life.

- Children with challenges may inadvertently present nonverbal cues that others assume to be deceptive and harboring harmful or negative intent.

- Each of the four major challenges discussed in this book potentially not only causes problems reading social cues, but also can stigmatize individuals as different and increase vulnerability to low self-esteem and bullying.

5

Reasons for Missing Social Cues

PHYSICAL DISABILITY—COMPENSATION (NO. 2 OF 11): "WHAT? HUH?"

I crept toward the chalkboard. OK, now I can read it. Then, in the fourth grade, I got my first glasses. Wow! I can read the board from the back of the room, without squinting! Individuals often develop intuitive compensations to make up for their challenges, whether they recognize that they have a challenge. I thought fuzzy was just how things looked. Many of Jerry's unusual behaviors were not only consequential to, but also intuitive compensations for, AS—the first of many reasons for missing social cues. Intuitive compensations for a physical disability or challenge may include tipping one's head or ears toward sounds, scanning left to right for limited peripheral vision, a deeper sniff to distinguish olfactory cues. The intuitive strategies may work relatively well. However, intuitive strategies that children come up with to compensate for disabilities may be stressful and risk misinterpretation. The teacher may think creeping toward the chalkboard is fidgeting. Or strategies may be ineffective and lead to even more stress and misinterpretation. A *Florida Today* article (Best, 2007) described a young girl named Kelsey Guyan. Teacher, peer, and her own perceptions of her abilities were largely negative. Finally an eye examination revealed that Kelsey had strabismus (commonly known as cross-eyed). Vision therapy taught her to use different parts of her brain for focus and mental concentration. As a result, her headaches and nausea went away. She got "smarter"! Unidentified physical disabilities or difficulties, specifically vision or hearing problems, can cause the miss or misinterpretation of social cues. Getting help for nonvisible disabilities, however, may be stigmatizing and increase children's chances of being victimized. Glasses, crutches, or other equipment reveal disabilities, identifying children as different. "Four eyes!" "Gimp!" Being sent to resource classes may have similar effects on children with LD or other special education issues. Adults must be aware that receiving extra help in school is predictive of a child being bullied (Carter & Spencer, 2006, p. 14). They should therefore be prepared to set boundaries and expectations with classmates along with helping the child in need.

CROSS-CULTURAL ISSUES— CROSS-CULTURAL EDUCATION (NO. 3 OF 11): "SO THAT'S WHAT YOU MEAN!"

"Don, you want the last piece of pie?" "No thanks," he replied. So, I ate it. Later, to his girlfriend, Don admitted, "I wanted that last piece. I thought Ronald was going to offer it to me again, that he'd insist I take it." She laughed, "Nope, with Ronald, you only get one chance!" Don was used to a social-cultural exchange that, in response to an offer, called for polite refusal by the guest, polite insistence by the host, repeated polite refusal followed by repeated polite insistence for a couple of additional rounds, whereupon, the guest graciously accepts. Such propriety around courtesy cues occurs in many ethnic or familial cultures, but not in my kitchen. Don, who was Japanese-American, had mistakenly assumed a socially defined courtesy or ritual from his background leading to his acceptance of the last piece of pie. However, I had asked, "Don, you want the last piece of pie?" as a literal question. He said no, so, I literally ate it! Was I culturally callous? Not in my culture. Cross-cultural education regarding social cues, courtesies, and rituals clarifies communication. Then next time he was over and I offered Don the last piece of a chocolate cake, he immediately responded, "Yes!" Successful cross-cultural education!

Everyone is served through purposeful cross-cultural education that promotes learning social cues. This involves not only the "what" of another culture—the behavior or expectations—but also the "why" of another culture. In other words, how does the behavior or expectations serve the contextual demands of individuals' and the community's functioning? One of the challenges of diversity is learning about the cultural norms of a group and the assumptions about communication and behavior. Any response or interaction is based on an individual's cultural training, which may be different from another individual's experiences. Individuals may share experiences such as historical experiences (for example, the

Depression or the Cold War), economic experiences (poverty), societal experiences (Puerto Rico community), educational experiences (college, or within that, an Ivy League experience), familial experiences (the Mah household), and so forth. Shared experience would tend to lead to shared common norms. Shared challenges also may result in fairly distinctive cultures, such as deaf culture, a term "developed in the 1970s to give utterance to the belief that Deaf communities contained their own ways of life mediated through their sign languages" (Ladd, 2003, p. xvii). Teachers should be aware that LD, ADHD, AS, or gifted abilities may also create distinctive cultural attitudes, values, beliefs, and behaviors mediated by individuals' common struggles for survival. Others who may not be familiar with such cultures may not understand what certain communications or behaviors mean and may respond or react inappropriately.

OVERSTIMULATION—DE-STRESS (NO. 4 OF 11): "I'M TIRED. I DON' WANNA HAVE FUN!"

Many parents keep their children active. The weekdays may be filled with piano lessons, sports, dance, Kumon tutoring, plus weekends with additional practice and performances, and electronic stimulation with MP3 players, text messaging, computers, video games. Classroom activity adds to the stimulation, especially with increasing demands for standards, test preparation, and testing. Too much enrichment or fertilizer doesn't help a plant grow, but burns and cripples it. Failure to recognize accumulation of stress or to know how to appropriately release it creates overwhelmed or overstimulated children. Overstimulation could interfere with a child's ability to recognize facial, tonal, or body language cues. Teachers can reduce stimulation through cutting back on activities, facilitating stress release, changing the tone and atmosphere of certain class periods, or incorporating quiet meditative times. In addition, some children arrive to school already "loaded" with stress: family strife, lack of sleep, chronic illness, developmentally inappropriate behavior demands, and so forth, along with other challenges, including experiences among the four target groups. Relatively minor stimulation such as fluorescent lights, tastes, smells, sounds, and dust floating in sunlight can become overwhelming to some children. For example, Attwood (2006) says that people with AS often describe feeling a sensation of sensory overload not readily apparent to others.

> There can be an under- or over-reaction to the experience of pain and discomfort, and the sense of balance, movement perception and body orientation can be unusual. One or several sensory systems can be affected such that everyday sensations are perceived as unbearably intense or apparently not perceived at all. Parents are often bewildered as to why these sensations are

intolerable or not noticed, while the person with Aspergers syndrome is equally bewildered as to why other people do not have the same level of sensitivity. (p. 272)

Overwhelmed people lose focus, becoming more likely to be surprised by circumstances and situations that others notice. Bullies like ambush. Preoccupied victims are less likely to resist or resist effectively. In the classroom, many teachers constantly monitor the level of overall stimulation among children and individual children. Within a relatively short time, children who get overwhelmed may act out. Teacher management of classroom stimulation should include helping children self-manage their individual stimulation.

DENIAL—ALLEVIATE FEAR
(NO. 5 OF 11): "NAH, NAH, NAH!"

Fingers in ears, eyes closed, and chatting "No, no, *no!*" children sometimes try to block out whatever seems intolerable. Individuals may find ugly or challenging things or experiences too much to handle. Losses and pain may be emotionally or psychologically devastating—too much, too intense. Denial is one of the primary defense mechanisms.

> When people are confronted with circumstances they find to be a threat, they often deny association or involvement with any aspect of the situation. Young children are often caught in the act of lying (denial) when they are accused of eating cookies right before dinner or making a mess in the bathroom. Examples in adulthood include denying a drinking or gambling problem. Any stimulus perceived to be a threat to the integrity of one's identity can push the button to deny involvement or knowledge. At a conscious level, the person truly believes he or she is innocent and sees nothing wrong with the behavior. (Seaward, 2002, p. 84–85)

Social cues can also be purposely ignored or denied. Recognizing that someone is uncomfortable or unhappy with them may require acknowledging something too emotionally or psychologically challenging. It feels too embarrassing. Some children cannot handle the realization that they cannot please everyone, cannot risk being wrong or getting into trouble, or cannot admit being "uncool." Denying a challenge or giftedness can come out of fear of being declared "weird" or "messed up." Adults need to support children around any issues that cause them to deny problems. Adults can point out children's other competencies, but the major emphasis would be that the challenges do not define children's inherent or total worth. In addition, a child may prefer to suffer victimization and deny it rather than admitting one's impotence. Being labeled a "wimp," a "doormat," or other label of helpless victimhood is too disturbing. Suffering in silence becomes the outcome of denial, which keeps victims isolated, increasing their vulnerability to being further bullied. Adults need to remove the option to suffer in silence. That is also known as being responsible teachers or adults!

ANXIETY—STABILIZE AND SECURE (NO. 6 OF 11): "WHAT? WHERE? WATCH OUT? WHERE? NOW? OH NO!"

Fear is specific, such as being afraid of snakes or of heights. Anxiety, however, develops without a specific source or object to fear. As a result, anxiety is without specific remedy. While individuals can avoid snakes or heights, anxious individuals cannot remove their amorphous sources of vague unpredictable fear. Normal fears are eliminated or reduced with frequent positive experiences. Reassurance, support, and positive experiences and outcomes do not readily relieve habitually anxious people. Normal anxiety is time-constrained to facilitate identifying and responding to the immediate demands of day-to-day life. Anticipating foreseeable issues among social contacts, normal anxiety prompts scanning for social cues to mood and intent. However, overanxious people stay in constant states of anxiety. They become hypersensitive and hypervigilant. Hypervigilance expends energy scanning unnecessarily in relatively benign situations. Hypersensitivity interprets neutral social cues as threatening. Anticipating ominous outcomes to innocent cues, hypervigilant and hypersensitive individuals err by being overcautious and overly negative. When teachers can create predictable, stable, and secure classroom environments and facilitate predictable interactions and relationships, children's anxiety is reduced. Unfortunately, some children may come into the classroom with persistent anxiety from chaotic and adverse family environments. In such cases, collaboration between teachers and parents may be necessary to reduce anxiety.

LD, ADHD, AS, and giftedness may exacerbate environmental causes of anxiety. Prior failures make children hypersensitive and hypervigilant to new frustration. For example, Connor (1999) describes this dynamic with children with AS.

> Problems with "tolerance" include a sensory and emotional oversensitivity, such that feelings are sometimes overwhelming even if they cannot be expressed or even understood, and a fear of other people or of being found unable to know what to do. . . . [T]here may be a focus upon a particular interest at the exclusion of all

others, an acute anxiety (albeit irrational) about a range of stimuli, and a possibility that other people's words or actions can spark off some unintended action. (Improving Learning Opportunities in Secondary Settings section, ¶ 3)

Children with special needs may be unaware of how their challenges affect perception and functioning. They may be unable to alter behaviors and may experience bad things happening repeatedly. If children anticipate something negative happening again, it reignites anxiety, which in turn intensifies negative behaviors. Further failure exacerbates the anxiety-failure-anxiety-failure cycle. Resultant behavior may destabilize the environment, which frustrates adults and heightens anxiety for everyone, including the already anxious child. Hypervigilance and hypersensitivity create the anxious vulnerability that tends to attract predatory bullies. Intervention involves breaking the cycles of anxiety and failure. Teachers can do this in the classroom by establishing concrete predictable routines and providing consistency in as many ways as possible. To do so, teachers must identify how children's challenges create anxiety. Specific processes can then be developed to alleviate an individual's anxiety and increase success.

NEUROSIS—REALITY FILTER OR CHECK (NO. 7 OF 11): "THAT WAS THEN, AND THIS IS THEN."

"Here, puppy, puppy." Pheromones emit. "Hi, puppy," a kind stranger slowly reaches a hand to pet the dog. The dog cringes reflexively and then snaps at the hand. All intentions and cues given indicated the stranger in this situation was not dangerous. But the dog's master had reached down and then smacked its head . . . many times. The dog misinterpreted the stranger's gentle cues as "Here we go again," and expected another smack on the head. Instincts and intuition based on prior experiences alter interpretation of cues and prediction of current or future situations. Perceptions become distorted to become fit expectations. Neuroses come from very negative prior experiences. Neuroses are anxious assumptions that previous bad outcomes are applicable to new situations. For example, previous punishment from upset adults can cause children to anticipate punishment from an upset but nurturing teacher. Similar misinterpretations may occur when receiving other children's social cues of aggression, discomfort, anger, and so forth. Children need an abundance of positive reparative experiences to countermand an abundance of previous negative experiences. Teachers can facilitate frequent reality checks regarding cues of classmates to counter neurotic filters. If teachers understand the patterns children have experienced, they can overtly assert the current reality. For example, if a child anticipates being punished, a teacher may say, "I'm not going to punish you. I'm telling you what to do instead. Do it and it'll be OK." Teachers may be able to recognize a neurotic reaction. Neurotic reactions that lead to common neurotic verbal responses include the following:

Being defensive: "I didn't do nuthin'!"

Projection: "You're the one who's mad!"

Misinterpreting intent: "They're always being mean to me!"

Making accusations: "They never let me play!"

Some individuals' personal histories cause them to perceive that past negative experiences are repeating themselves. Teachers can recognize certain terminology children use to assert neurotic interpretations of reality. They can then provide a reality check for children regarding the implication of inevitability. Reality filters may initially target refuting the absolute modifiers: *always, never, must be,* and *all the time,* and contesting the assumption of unjust repetition conveyed by the word *again.* These absolute modifiers assert unalterable doom. Teachers can prompt children to accept their partial influence, power, and control to affect what happens. Teachers can recognize when children are predicting doom when they hear children expressing with declarative terminology such as the following:

"It must be . . ."

"I will be . . ."

"They must be going to . . ."

" . . . always . . ."

" . . . never . . ."

" . . . all the time . . ."

Teachers should instruct and guide children to substitute terminology that acknowledges potential problems but still allows for other possibilities and outcomes:

"It might be . . ."

"I might be . . ."

"They might be going to . . ."

" . . . could be or not!"

" . . . sometimes . . ."

" . . . too often . . ."

The words *sometimes* and *too often* assert displeasure without asserting doom. Hope is allowed! They imply the possibility of increasing positive frequency while decreasing negative frequency. If children with challenges are not appropriately supported, negative experiences may dominate their consciousness. Adults can help children by identifying even limited power, control, and competence versus accepting their neurotic self-definition as victims. Teachers can do this in the classroom, while other adults may do this in other situations. This is a critical first step to empowerment and growth.

DISASSOCIATION—TRAUMA WORK (NO. 8 OF 11): "*CLICK* . . . THIS STATION IS NO LONGER BROADCASTING . . . OR RECEIVING."

Denial is the cognitive blocking of intolerable experiences or feelings. Neurosis is the anxious interpretation that things will turn out badly again. Disassociation, on the other hand, occurs when experiences are too devastating to be endured. Unconscious processes turn off memory, disconnect individuals from feelings altogether, or block their response to triggers or stimulation. A single devastating incident or ongoing experiences such as witnessing or experiencing violence or chronic physical, sexual, or emotional abuse, may render feelings or thoughts beyond a person's conscious tolerance. Teachers should be aware that some children are more vulnerable to a traumatic experience. They may be more likely to experience ongoing stresses because of their challenges. With disassociation, cues may become triggers or stressors if they are similar to those of an original trauma. As a result, traumatized individuals freeze. Beyond missing social cues, even more obvious communications are missed. The lights are on, but no one is in. Individuals may have traumatic experiences from outside the classroom or chronic victimization that can create the possibility of disassociation in response to triggers that other children handle readily. Stressors may be discipline by teachers, academic demands, or social requirements. Teachers can anticipate that conflict situations, picking members for teams, birthday invitations and celebrations, field trips, tests, using the restroom, and so forth may be potential triggers depending on individual history. Getting history from previous teachers and parents helps identify potential triggers, and teachers can prepare children for the cues. For example, teachers can announce, "I'm about to tell you something that sounds scary, but you will be OK doing it." Adding a hug or holding a child uses touch to maintain emotional connection, which may preclude or reduce disassociation.

LEARNING DISABILITIES—COMPENSATION (NO. 9 OF 11): "TRYING HARD, HARDER, AND HARDER . . ."

What is said:

> First, pick a partner. Second, get the blocks from the tub. Third, open your workbook to page 3. Then, make a structure that copies the picture on page 3. After that, make a structure of your own creation. Last, make a picture of your creation.

What is heard:

> First, pick a partner. Second, tick tick tick [from the clock]. Tick, open your workbook . . . rustling pages. Then, make a . . . *Stop it, Bill* . . . on page 3. After that, make a structure of your . . . giggling [from the back of the room]. Last, . . . rustling pages . . . tick tick tick . . . creation.

Anxiety, neuroses, disassociation, and other issues that complicate reading social cues can arise from children's struggles with LD. Sometimes teachers' learning and teaching styles do not match the learning styles of children or don't adequately compensate for LD. As a result, children can have difficulty in learning and communication as well as with social interactions or relationships. Teachers need to evaluate their own teaching styles for potential fit or misfit with particular children. For example, teachers can have primarily auditory teaching styles that mismatch the abilities of children with auditory processing issues who may be strong visual learners. Auditory or visual instruction may not connect well with motor-kinesthetic strengths characteristic of children with LD or ADHD. Instruction from a teacher-directed versus a child-centered or initiated orientation may or may not fit various children's abilities to manage impulsive energy. Some teachers provide a lot of structure that some children find stabilizing. Other children may find it stifling. Open-ended exploratory projects may ignite some student's creativity, while causing others to flounder for lack of sufficient structure. As a result of teachers failing to compensate for learning differences, some children may miss social cues and respond inappropriately in class.

Classmates, frustrated or offended by a child's failure to understand and respond appropriately, label him or her "rude," "mean," or "weird." In the example above, an auditory listening disability draws attention to background sounds (clock ticking, paper rustling, kids' noises, etc.) rather than on the foreground sounds (teacher's voice). Missing instructions leads to numerous problems. Children may end up doing the project incorrectly and act out to hide ignorance. Even though children try hard to attend, many emphases from nonverbal facial, tonal, or body language cues are missed. Other learning disabilities can also complicate reading social cues. For example, instructions are heard but inefficiently processed into short-term memory, creating "forgetting." Some children have inefficient retrieval of information from cognitive storage, which takes more time and concentration, making one oblivious to continuing cues from the others. Individuals with dyslexia may struggle to recognize letters that are "mirrors" of each other (*b* and *d*, *p* and *q*, *M* and *W*, *Z* and *N*,) resulting in missing or misinterpreting social cues. Or an LD may directly challenge recognition of cues causing significant negative social consequences. Whitney (2002) says,

> Children with NLD [nonverbal learning disorder] are frequently the target of bullies. Because they take things literally, because they are so trusting, and because they rarely tattle, they are the perfect victims. Often they can't tell the difference between bullying and friendly banter or dangerous intentions. Unfortunately, bullies know exactly how to mistreat others without letting grown-ups see them. A child with NLD won't be able to read the subtle cues that tell the bully the teacher isn't paying attention, so he is likely to assume the teacher sees the bully's behavior and condones it. Frequently the teacher hasn't seen the bully's behavior and the teacher only sees when the child with NLD reacts to the bully's taunts. A child with NLD will react whether the adult is around or not. (p. 36)

Children with LD or any challenge often have an intuitive approach to learning problems that directs them to try harder. They try harder with what has already proven ineffective or inefficient. Trying hard and harder may sometimes have marginal benefit, but such children often do not develop successful compensations on their own. Teachers often need to teach children specific compensations for LD: auditory challenges with visual compensations, visual difficulties through auditory strengths, and so forth.

ATTENTION DEFICIT HYPERACTIVITY DISORDER (AND ATTENTION DEFICIT DISORDER)—FOCUS (NO. 10 OF 11): "ATTENTION WANDERS . . ."

"And Marc gets involved with his guitar," complains Debra. Marc watches her. Gradually, his gaze and attention wanders to the window where a branch sways in the wind. "And it's just hard," Debra says tearfully, head bowed, and hands clasped. Marc watches the branch. "And he just doesn't care!" Debra snaps, giving Marc a death stare! "Huh? What?" Marc is busted! But he does care. His attention wanes despite his best intentions during Debra's expansive discourse. It wanders just as it did in elementary school when the teacher lectured. ADHD and attention deficit disorder (ADD) share the common issue of high distractibility. With wandering attention, someone like Marc misses subtleties of cues. Subsequently he cannot respond to the missed messages: tears, bowed head, clasping hands, and especially, the quavering voice. The golden rule of couplehood is violated: "If you really love me, you would be completely attentive and responsive to my every need, no matter how subtle!" The golden rule of relationships (teacher-student, friend-friend) regarding respect is virtually the same. "If you respect me as the teacher (or friend), you'd listen and respond to me!" That's why Marc got into so much trouble in elementary school. When Debra realized that the golden rule was not immune to ADHD influences or a myriad of other emotional, psychological, cultural, and processing issues, she accepted that Marc's ADHD made paying attention difficult for him. Becoming distracted happened despite his loving her. She then accepted helping Marc focus to keep his attention. Marc took responsibility that attention was a critical challenge to being successful in his relationship and elsewhere. With practice, he improved his recognition of her underlying messages as conveyed by nonverbal cues. Like Marc, children with ADHD or ADD care desperately that teachers and classmates like them. Yet they often fail to keep focused on others' words and end up displeasing others. When Debra thought Marc was dismissive, she snapped at and badly treated him. Classmates, when hurt by inattention they interpret as dismissive, may feel entitled to be hurtful back. They wreck vengeful retribution by ostracizing, teasing, and aggression against the perceived transgressors. Unaware of their transgressions, ADHD or ADD children experience negativity that seemingly comes out of nowhere. Mistreatment seems completely unjustified. This may prompt retaliatory behaviors by ADHD or ADD children, which in turn prompts further retaliation. When teachers recognize such negative behavior cycles between children, they can try to break them with education about cues, boundaries, and consequences.

INTOXICATION AND SUBSTANCE ABUSE—SOBRIETY (NO. 11 OF 11): "COMMON ADVERSE EFFECTS . . ."

The eleventh reason, intoxication and substance abuse, might seem most relevant to teenagers and adults. However, many children are on medication. Medication that has either a sedative or a stimulant effect may affect alertness and focus. Children's cough medicine may include chemicals such as dextromethorphan with possible side effects including dizziness, lightheadedness, drowsiness, nervousness, and restlessness (MedlinePlus, 2008). Albuterol sulfate (brand name, Ventolin HFA), an asthma medication, may have a stimulant effect on some children (GlaxoSmithKline, 2008). Parents need to advise teachers of any medication taken by children that potentially may cause unanticipated attention or hyperactivity or other problems. With these warnings, teachers can note and inform parents of any behavior changes in medicated children. It appears that children suffering emotional distress, at ever decreasingly younger ages, may access alcohol, over-the-counter drugs susceptible to abuse, and recreational illicit drugs to self-medicate. Giedd (2003) surveyed research and found the diagnoses of ADHD and substance abuse occur together more frequently than expected by chance alone. The National Center on Addiction and Substance Abuse at Columbia University (2000) examined the link between LD and substance abuse and found

> adolescents with low self-esteem may use drugs for self-medication purposes—to counter negative feelings associated with social rejection and school failure. . . . Some specialists believe that people with ADHD medicate themselves with drugs such as alcohol, marijuana, heroin, pain medication, caffeine, nicotine and cocaine to counter feelings of restlessness. (p. 9)

Self-medication occurs among many depressed or anxious individuals. Ritalin, a common medication for ADHD symptoms and easy to obtain, has been used as a recreational or self-medicating drug among children (Chiauzzi, 2007). Ritalin has an effect similar to cocaine or methamphetamine when taken at higher dosages, snorted nasally when crushed, or dissolved to be taken intravenously. Children with challenges may turn to alcohol or other self-medicating behaviors to counter their painful experiences. Self-mutilation or self-injury might be considered forms of self-medication. For example, cutting, trichotillomania (pulling one's hair out), or other self-injuries trigger a physiological response that includes a whole canopy of chemical responses, including chemicals that numb not just physical pain but also painful emotions. Timofeyev, Sharff, Burns, and Outterson (2002) suggest that in addition to dopamine, "endogenous opioids have also been linked to self-mutilation. The biological reinforcement theory suggests that the pain from self-mutilation may cause the production of endorphins (endogenous opioids) that reduce dysphoria. A cycle is formed in which the habitual self-mutilator will hurt themselves in order to feel better" (Biological Explanations section, ¶ 3). Workaholism, gambling, spending, compulsive exercising, over- or undereating, obsessive-compulsive behaviors, and so forth can also activate biological processes for emotional self-medication. Teachers may discover that behavioral compulsions or acting out may be the first and only observable indications of individuals' depression, anxiety, or victimization and should make appropriate referrals for such children.

Teachers may encounter all of the reasons for missing social cues—sometimes within one year and one class! Children frequently behave in an inappropriate or mysterious way. Children's vulnerability to misbehavior may vary due to missing social cues because of one or more of these eleven reasons. Often several of these reasons coexist to compromise a single child's functioning. These conceptualizations may guide intervention.

Chapter Highlights

- Intuitive strategies that children come up with to compensate for disabilities may be stressful and risk misinterpretation.

- Some children arrive to school already "loaded" with stress: family strife, lack of sleep, chronic illness, developmentally inappropriate behavior demands, and so forth, along with other challenges.

- Intervention needs to happen with or without the "permission" of the victimized. Such intervention becomes an assertion of adult commitment to healthy life and opposition to victimization.

- Anticipating ominous outcomes to innocent cues, hypervigilant and hypersensitive individuals err by being overcautious and overly negative.

- Reality filters may initially target refuting the absolute modifiers: *always, never, must be,* and *all the time,* and contesting the assumption of unjust repetition conveyed by the word *again.*

- Individuals may have traumatic experiences from outside the classroom or chronic victimization that can create the possibility of disassociation in response to triggers that other children handle readily.

- Teachers need to evaluate their own teaching styles for potential fit or misfit with particular children and their learning styles.

- Teachers may discover that behavioral compulsions or acting out may be the first and only observable indications of individuals' depression, anxiety, or victimization.

6

The Victim Dynamic

WHY DO YOU PICK UP CRYING BABIES?

Victimization may happen at home and continue at school or start and persist in school. Once victimized, some children are repeatedly bullied. Those who develop a victim personality may gravitate to dysfunctional strategies and mentalities that perpetuate being victimized. Adults may inadvertently contribute to a victim personality by how they support these children. Physically and emotionally available, trustworthy adults ordinarily help children develop a sense of survivability. Survivability is strongly related to resiliency and comes from a core of secure attachment.

Why do you pick up crying babies? They are in distress over discomfort, hunger, being startled, and so forth. Babies in distress who are not attended to slide into despair. The difference can be heard in their cry. Babies do not know how to self-soothe. Caregivers pick up babies. As babies are soothed, they learn how to self-soothe from the caregiver's model, to rock themselves gently the way the caregivers rocked them, to caress themselves around their faces and bodies the way caregivers did. Babies eventually learn to murmur the gentle nurturing sounds that they have heard from caregivers.

Babies that learn how to self-soothe become children, teenagers, and adults who know how to self-soothe. The reverse is also true. Children who do not know how to self-soothe will act out to gain negative attention. They take the negative attention because that is all they feel they can get. Teenagers and adults who do not know how to self-soothe may use alcohol, drugs, sex, food, self-injury, and any number of other dysfunctional behaviors in order to self-soothe. Teenagers and adults who do not know how to self-soothe often demand that others soothe them when they are in need. And if for some reason the other people fail to soothe them, they will lash out and punish them for their betrayal.

Why do you pick up crying babies? Because this is how they learn that in the big wide world, there is someone who cares that they are in distress. This is the fundamental behavior of all those wonderful attachment theories! Some people advocate letting babies "cry it out" because they are focusing on a practical problem or behavior, such as sleeping for more than a few hours. Restless sleep is a legitimate problem to be handled in any number of ways, but should not interfere with developing secure attachment. When teachers and other adults focus solely on solving a problematic behavior, they risk missing that a cry of discomfort also is a cry of need. If adults don't respond to the cry, the "cry it out" advocates are correct . . . the baby will stop crying because beyond the cry being a cry of discomfort, it also becomes a cry of hope. When babies, children, teens, and adults lose hope, they don't cry out anymore. Children and adults need to be nurtured and supported in order to develop a sense of survivability. Most adult caregivers including teachers know this instinctively and try to soothe children in distress.

Caregiving adults need to be aware that they may overcompensate and inadvertently teach children that they won't survive, creating children used to and dependent upon being rescued. Teachers need to constantly evaluate children and situations to determine how available they should be. They need to carefully offer appropriate support, while sometimes withholding it. To do so appropriately, they must be attuned to the specific challenges of individual children. The secure attachment that is so critical to healthy children needs to be balanced with facilitating children's strength and skills. Children who learn to self-soothe are more likely to also learn how to take care of themselves. Secure attachment or basic trust is the foundation of children's independence. Children cannot develop a sense of survivability critical to success without having opportunities to competently handle challenges on their own. This sometimes includes having to deal with not being OK. What starts out somewhat innocently to support children can become a huge problem because of lost opportunities.

> [Whomp!] Ow! I must have tripped. . . . Ow! [Peek] Where's teacher? She looking? Help me! I'm gonna die! Hurry up! Teeeecher! I'm lying here on the ground . . . dying! Save me! I don't know what to do . . . [louder] Tuh-tuh-EEE- CHER! OW! OWWW!

Everyone recognizes dramatic children who play up and exaggerate their minor bump or scratch. Most of them give up recruiting adult salvation or intervention when sage parents and teachers recognize their manipulations and set appropriate boundaries. However, some children cannot seem to give up the act. Furthermore, for some children, it is not really an act. They are being victimized regularly. Victimized children initially draw caring adults and classmates to help them. However, people may find it difficult to keep liking the perpetual victims. Victims often draw others' hearts to them only to break them. Despite initial empathy for them, the constant victim's seeming inability to learn, change, and stop being victimized becomes increasingly frustrating to those who care. These victims never seem to be able to take help or guidance to become more successful. Concern for victims unable to change can create a sense of impotence for helpers. Would-be rescuers end up feeling helpless just like the victims they seek to help. With their own doubts ignited about power and control, rescuers often can become angry with perpetual victims. Parent may become angry with their children. Teachers may become angry with their students who get victimized. Guilt-ridden, such adults go back to help, but repeatedly fail to get victims to help themselves. Their sense of competency as nurturers or as loving, caring, and supportive adults is damaged.

VICTIMIZED BY VICTIMS

Feeling victimized by perpetual victims, people begin avoiding them. Would-be helpers need to realize they might inadvertently reward perpetual victims for their helplessness. The victim dynamic "benefits" the victims. Victim personalities appear to be highly incompetent, but actually are extremely competent at being victims. Being a victim becomes an effective, though dysfunctional, way to gain power and control. Children with any of a variety of challenges are often extremely intuitive. A five-year-old with Down syndrome had figured out adults did not expect her to respond quickly to simple commands. Told to get off the swing to go inside since recess was over, Beth kept swinging and stared blankly at the teacher. Her visage seemed to state, "I don't know what you want." She expected the teacher (me) to repeat the command several times, as adults probably had done a hundred times before. Eventually, she would comply when the adults would finally get insistent. Instead of repeating that pattern, immediately I told her firmly, "You heard what I said!" She quickly jumped off the swing and went inside. Down syndrome? Yes. Stupid? Not by a long shot! The blank look and noncompliance had worked for Beth many times before to gain power and control from less cynical adults! The practice of helplessness while gaining superficial benefits can have significant negative life consequences. For example, Bridget described her lifetime of horrific experiences: old and current family issues, toxic relationships with abusive men, oppressive work situations. A strong and pervasive sense of helplessness emanated from her. I could practically hear the violin music! Empathy alone would not help her and will not help victimized children either. Consciously and subconsciously, Bridget was asking me to change into my "gallant knight" armor and ride to the rescue!

After fifteen minutes, I said gently, "You're so good at being helpless." Bridget was shocked, "What!? . . . What do you mean?" She had anticipated the classic "Oh, poor baby" response that would have confirmed her helplessness. Getting attention through other people's sympathy was her power and control strategy. I continued, "You're very good at being depressed, being a victim." Stunned, she said, "What do you mean?" I explained, "When you are depressed and helpless, people, especially friends, take care of you. As a miserable victim, you get cut a lot of slack and get help from others. You get a lot of power and control that way. By being hopeless, you avoid taking risks, avoid challenging yourself. You keep yourself in an uncomfortable but familiar world of quiet desperation. Being helpless works for you." Bridget's response? She said, "Oh."

REVERSING THE DUAL THEORY OF FRAILTY

What I call the "Dual Theory of Frailty" asserts first that the individual is too frail to handle being told the truth. Conversely, telling an individual the truth asserts she is strong enough to hear and then deal with reality. The second part of the theory would have been that I, as the helper (or the teacher or the parent), was also too frail, incapable of managing her if she became distraught or confused. Withholding truth would have implied that I didn't trust either of us to be strong, resilient, or resourceful enough to undergo the process of growth and change. To reverse the negative messages of this theory, teachers and parents require confidence, clarity, and skills to challenge children's victim tendencies. This is particularly challenging as adults must balance empowerment with sensitivity for children's vulnerabilities.

Refusing to believe in the Dual Theory of Frailty, I therefore instead told Bridget the truth. I challenged her long-term habitual means to gain a sense of illusionary power and control. When children get adults to save them, they also gain a sense of illusionary power and control—in the moment. Bridget learned that childhood victimization had led her to dysfunctional patterns of hopelessness and helplessness and then to the victim dynamic and seeking rescue. She began to explore and experiment with healthier and more affirmative ways to gain power and control. Over the next eighteen months, she changed jobs and took some risks. Eventually, Bridget met a nice guy, developed a romantic relationship (with plenty of anxiety!), and became engaged. She stopped being a victim and is currently working on the "happily ever after" part!

HOW VICTIMS ARE CREATED

Some children develop victim personalities from being victimized at home by family members. However, some come from very nurturing families without any hint of bullying. While Marano (1995) states that victims tend to be sensitive, nonviolent, and nonaggressive, they do not become victims without other important experiences. Victims also tend to have very close relationships with their parents. When adults, especially parents, realize that children have some special needs, they often respond with more support, involvement, and vigilance. Closeness, involvement, and vigilance may promote positive development. However, they may also be expressed in ways that backfire and disempower children. The victim personality is developed by protective actions that inadvertently prevent children from developing skills, such as assertiveness, negotiation, and compromise, that are necessary to handle confrontations with others, especially with bullies. Rather than "Have no fear, protectors are here!" it becomes "Stay in fear, protectors must get here . . . or else!"

Some children are affected not by learning differences, a processing issue, or a physical challenge, but from overprotective parents and well-intended overcompensation. Some adults assume and project that children are overwhelmed, vulnerable, or incapable due to youth, personality, or some difference that results in insufficient skills, resources, and resiliency to handle conflicts. Within these families, children may be protected from siblings' aggression or any other discomfort. Continued rescues from adults' fear of children's vulnerability can become a self-fulfilling prophecy. Outside their nurturing loving families in the real world, children find that others won't do anything for them like Mommy or Daddy. Adults who continually rescue children steal from them opportunities to learn how to handle conflict. Thus children do not develop the resiliency necessary to deal with stress, frustration, failure, and emotional distress. Without opportunities to practice and develop skills and strength, children become more and more vulnerable to other children's aggressive behavior. At school, since parents cannot be available, children who are used to being rescued expect teachers to become the designated rescuers. Some teachers, if intent on protecting children, may unknowingly perpetuate the victim personality. Realistically, teachers cannot catch and intervene with every aggressive act among students. They cannot realistically be perfect monitors of all potential harmful social interactions among children. Children who are frequently victimized compensate for inconsistent or erratic teacher intervention by becoming extremely vigilant and scanning for any bully's approach. They frequently interrupt activity to scan the horizon, as moments of calm are broken by alarm. They show dilated and widened eyes, facial and postural tension, and nervous motions. Intended to prevent ambush, anxious vulnerability makes them readily identifiable for bullies looking for easy prey. Adults must intervene quickly and assertively when circumstances or individuals are overwhelming or dangerous. Other times, children must be required to draw upon and learn skills, resources, and resiliency, despite how difficult it may be. Adults must manage their own anxiety about failing victimized children to best serve them with encouragement, training, empowerment, or protection when necessary. Children need to be challenged, stretched, and succeed or fail, and yet survive. Adults must be able to watch children struggle, even suffer to handle stress, conflicts, and intrusive or exploitative people, including bullies.

Some disabilities are skill or process weaknesses that can be improved with training. Other disabilities can be minimized or compensated for by activating and enhancing other abilities. Children's challenges sometimes make it difficult to learn necessary compensations. Verbal instruction or a verbal list of things to do in a conflict situation, for example, may not work well with children with distraction, auditory processing issues, and so on. Prompting responses to facial cues may be ineffective without compensating for children who have difficulty recognizing social cues because of AS or certain visual or auditory learning disabilities. Gifted children may get caught up in the conceptual stimulation of conflict principles and fail to integrate and activate concrete conflict resolution behavior. They would need to be guided through their theorizing toward following through with specific behaviors in actual situations. Generic interventions not attuned to specific children's challenges can make things worse. Stepping in too readily reinforces avoidance of dealing with problems. Avoidance may already be a tendency of children with challenges to deal with problems. Children with significant challenges handling conflict in particular may be "supported" by overprotective adults into lifelong inabilities to handle bullies' aggression. Thus they may develop enduring victim personalities.

What are the skills that children need to have to handle aggression and bullying? Typical of many others' recommendations, Marano (1995) lists five things:

- A wise line of defense is avoidance. Know when to walk away. It is thoroughly adaptive behavior to avoid a bully. Being picked on is not character-building.
- Use humor to defuse a bully who may be about to attack. Make a joke: "Look, Johnny, lay off. I don't want you to be late for school."
- Tell the bully assertively, "Get a life. Leave me alone." And walk away. This may be the best defense for girls.
- Recruit a friend. Observers find that having a friend on the playground is one of the most powerful protectives, especially for boys.
- In general, seek out the friendly children and build friendships with them.

All these recommendations are appropriate with a big qualifying *if*. They can be effective *if* they can be activated. The negative side of the recommendation of avoidance may be that on its own, it supports increased anxious vulnerability. The fourth and fifth recommendations about friends can be problematic for a child who is already ostracized as a victim or deemed different or both. The second and third recommendations both require verbal skills that may be challenging for some children. Problems with verbal communication may be linked to aggression or other behavioral problems for children.

Aggression has been associated with low language proficiency as early as the second year of life and throughout the lifespan. Although language deficits are not sufficient or necessary correlates of aggressive behavior problems ... this has led to a consensus around the view that the link between language and behavior is functional, not spurious. (Dionne, 2005, p. 330)

Verbal fluency also becomes a means to avoid victimization. Verbal fluency is a key to gaining social fluency. Children that can tell a joke may deflect the aggressive or angry arousal of a bully into laughter. Verbally setting clear and compelling boundaries with substantial consequences may cause a bully to recalculate the gain versus cost of bullying. Verbally adept children tend to be better able to negotiate or "spar" with aggressive children through humor, setting boundaries, or problem solving. Verbal fluency also differentiates between assertive children who become social leaders versus those who may become aggressive bullies. Bullies use aggression to demonstrate power over others, but aggression and power are not synonymous. Aggression can be a means to use and achieve power, including achieving positions of leadership. However, there are other socially acceptable ways to be leaders by being assertive without necessarily being aggressive. Marano (1995) refers to boys who are aggressive, but don't get their way by physical aggression or verbal abuse. They assume leadership by establishing dominance through the socially appropriate skill of verbal fluency. Teachers can help children by modeling, teaching, prompting, and requiring development of verbal skills. Conflict resolution and mediation programs may be useful to teach specific verbalizations for assertiveness and boundary setting.

Chapter Highlights

- When teachers and other adults focus solely on solving a problematic behavior, they risk missing that a cry of discomfort also is a cry of need.
- Victim personalities appear to be highly incompetent, but actually are extremely competent at being victims. Being a victim becomes an effective, though dysfunctional, way to gain power and control.
- Teachers and parents require confidence, clarity, and skills to challenge children's victim tendencies. This is particularly challenging as adults must balance empowerment with sensitivity for children's vulnerabilities.
- The victim personality is developed by protective actions that inadvertently prevent children from developing skills, such as assertiveness, negotiation, and compromise, that are necessary to handle confrontations with others, especially with bullies.
- Adults must manage their own anxiety about failing victimized children to best differentially serve them with encouragement, training, and empowerment, or with protection when necessary.
- Generic interventions not attuned to specific children's challenges can make things worse.
- Verbal fluency also becomes a means to avoid victimization. Verbal fluency is a key to gaining social fluency.

7

Creating Bullies

A BLUSTERING, BROWBEATING PERSON

Children must develop greater personal power without forcing their will upon others. Charismatic and powerful individuals sometimes dominate and coerce others. The greater one's power, the greater one's responsibility to respect the rights and needs of others. Children who are immersed in a sense of helplessness may become aggressive in order to avoid further victimization. Adults often instinctively know that bullies have self-esteem issues, but forget that factor when they become antagonized from dealing with the bullying behavior. The desire to protect oneself and to deny further victimization should be considered strengths. This energy can be activated with appropriate guidance toward healthy self-empowerment. Unfortunately, some victimized children instead look to avenge humiliations. They decide that in a dog-eat-dog world, they must be the big dog. To avoid being bullied or to gain self-esteem, they may become bullies themselves. Who becomes a responsible leader and who becomes a tyrant? How are bullies created? Who are bullies? Flynt and Morton (2004) offer this definition of bullies:

> One definition of the term bully is "a blustering browbeating person; especially, one habitually cruel to others who are weaker." . . . Regardless of the source, most definitions of the term "bully" incorporate three distinct attributes. . . . First, the harassment of the victim occurs over an extended period of time. Second, the intent behind the harassment is meant to cause harm either mentally or physically to the victim. And finally, an imbalance of power is apparent. (Definitions section, ¶ 2)

Intimidating others may feel not only appropriate but also desirable for bullies who are bullied by parents. Adult bullies are compelling models for their children to emulate. However, well-intended nonbullying parents and later other adults can also raise bullies. These parents often then become such children's first victims! Their siblings, and eventually classmates and teachers, are next. Despite love and good intentions, misunderstanding of personalities and needs affecting psychosocial adjustment can result in children becoming bullies. Nansel et al. (2004) studied the relationship between bullying and psychosocial adjustment (emotional adjustment, relationships with classmates, and health problems) across twenty-five countries. They found that

> across all countries, involvement in bullying was associated with poorer psychosocial adjustment ($P < .05$). In all or nearly all countries, bullies, victims, and bully-victims reported greater health problems and poorer emotional and social adjustment. Victims and bully-victims consistently reported poorer relationships with classmates, whereas bullies and bully-victims reported greater alcohol use and weapon carrying. (p. 730)

They concluded, "The association of bullying with poorer psychosocial adjustment is remarkably similar across countries. Bullying is a critical issue for the health of youth internationally." Children with issues such as LD, ADHD, AS, and giftedness often suffer multiple challenging psychosocial adjustments. They might first come to a professional's attention not because of their learning challenges but when their parents seek relief from their little bully's tyranny in the home. As parents and teachers understand this dynamic, they can make adjustments to better guide children.

BULLIES, AGGRESSION, AND THE SEARCH FOR SELF-ESTEEM

Defense mechanisms, including denial, serve to avoid anxiety that would otherwise be overwhelming. Teachers may encounter parents who are in denial that their children are bullies. They may be protective of their children, including their children's reputations. If teachers can help parents understand the numerous negative consequences their children will suffer by becoming bullies, it may motivate parents to get past the shame and face reality. Teachers can help parents by focusing not only on behavior that needs to be eliminated, but also on how behavior change can have long-term positive consequences for their children. The teacher-parent alliance is essential in promoting character growth and change in children. Unable to distinguish among socially acceptable assertiveness and bullying, bullies' behavior and reputations create misery for others and themselves. From early on, bullies experience downward life spirals. In their research of third-, fourth-, and fifth-grade students, Glew et al. (2005) said that

> All of the groups involved in bullying were significantly more likely to be suspended or expelled; to feel unsafe, sad, and like they didn't belong at school; and to endorse cheating if they could get away with it compared with bystanders. Bullies . . . were more likely than bystanders to endorse carrying guns to school, beating up someone who started a fight, and smoking cigarettes. Non-responders were not more likely to say they felt sad, unsafe, or that they did not belong. (p. 1029)

Bullies are much more likely to become antisocial adults, have criminal problems, become batterers, child abusers, and tragically produce more bullies in next generation. Sourander et al. (2007) found in their longitudinal study that

> Boys who bully frequently in childhood are at elevated risk for recidivism and for committing violent, property, traffic, and drunk driving offenses in late adolescence. To illustrate this, 21.1% of frequent bully-victims and 15.9% of those with frequent bully-only status were recidivist offenders, compared with only 6.8% of those who did not exhibit frequent bullying behavior. Although frequent bullies and bully-victims composed only 8.8% of the total sample, they were responsible for 33.0% of all offenses during the 4-year period between the ages of 16 and 20 years, i.e., 8 to 12 years after the initial assessment. (p. 550)

Beyond delinquent and criminal behavior, bullying ends up harming learning, friendships, work, intimacy, income, and mental health.

> Childhood physical aggression is of particular concern as it is viewed as a precursor of physical and mental health problems such as, higher risk of alcohol and drug abuse, depression, suicide attempts, violent crimes and neglectful and abusive parenting. Furthermore, aggressive behavior in children and adolescents has been identified as a current major public health concern ranging from frequent bullying to violence and delinquency. (Tauscher-Wisniewski, 2006, p. 1398)

At best, people struggle to find sufficient compassion to like bullies. Classmates and teachers don't like to be around bullies unless the culture of the school gives social status to bullying behavior. Despite distorted self-images, social sanctions continually give bullies negative feedback. Others' reactions constantly remind bullies of their failure to live up to their ideal selves as powerful people. They lose power and control with continual restrictions from adults for their poor behavior.

Bullies are often socially incompetent, coming up short in all the four components of self-esteem.

- Significance: They don't get messages of worth from significant people. Being feared becomes a substitute for significance.
- Moral virtue: They fail to live up to their ideal selves as being omnipotent. Transitory domination and intimidation become substitutes for being socially accepted by others.
- Power and control: They are frequently out of control and subsequently lose power. Bullying others gives them only short-term illusions of being powerful.
- Competence: They fail in the areas they deem important to themselves. They are only competent at being bullies.

As a result, bullies' low self-esteem motivates their creation of a tenuous sense of worth based on aggression. Teachers can help such children gain self-esteem and, as a result, diminish their need to bully. It is important to support children's desire to gain success in each of the four components of self-esteem. Challenging and evolving these children's moral virtues, that is, their self-definition of who they should be, is critical. Bullies often bully to compensate for vulnerabilities in the other three components. As long as they feel they should be aggressive and intimidating, they will not be amenable to developing other approaches for interaction. If teachers set boundaries and apply consequences to bullying behavior, they can then also reframe the behavior as ineffective: "That not only is not OK, but it doesn't work for you." They can remind children that their bullying behavior loses rather than gains power, control, or social status: "You got fewer choices. Others don't like or respect you for your behavior." Then teachers can direct and guide them toward more appropriate behavior to satisfy their underlying needs. "If you want to have . . . then you can . . . instead. That's how you can be more powerful, have more friends, get more privileges." Some children need specific direction in what to do instead. This is particularly relevant when the negative responses have become habitual and driven by powerful emotions.

"WHO ARE YOU LOOKING AT!?"

Bullies possess a kind of paranoia where provocation is perceived without justification. "Who are you looking at!?" "Stop messing with me!" Barkley (2006) says,

Some evidence suggests that children with ADHD also encode social cues less well, express less optimism about future events, and generate few responses to problematic social situations than do disabled children . . . children with ADHD who are also aggressive or have ODD/CD [oppositional defiant disorder/conduct disorder] may display this same problem with encoding cues, but also manifest an additional tendency to over-interpret the actions of others toward them as actually having hostile intentions, and are therefore more likely to respond with aggressive counterattacks to minimal if any provocation. (p. 199)

The four target populations are vulnerable to misinterpretations of others' intent, which can prompt their retaliatory behaviors. People are often stunned when targeted by bullies' hostility for something they had not done or had done innocently. Paranoia distorts bullies' perception and interpretation of innocent comments and behavior. Bullies often do not see themselves negatively because it would be too threatening to their self-image. Thus they feel completely justified to retaliate aggressively. Aggression gets the last cookie or first place in line. Hostility intimidates classmates into silence, which is interpreted as permission to continue the negative behavior. Bullies anticipate only short-term outcomes without considering future consequences to themselves or others. "It gets me the ball now! Stupid kid is mad. So? Later, when I grow up? Baah! I got it!" Such "successes" build a fragile sense of self-esteem, locking them into patterns of aggressive and hostile responses, acceptable only to others similar to them. This social consequence becomes especially true for male bullies. Increasingly isolated, they hang out and socialize only with others like them. Unable to function among other children and tolerated only by other bullies, they form packs. This often is somewhat different for females because of gender role differences that will be discussed later.

"HUH? WHAT?"

Sometimes marginally skilled parents or teachers come up against difficult children with more intense and problematic personalities. The social, cultural, or financial environments may significantly compromise parents' ability to diligently attend to these children. In the classroom, testing, unpredictable and unexpected schedule changes, and classroom dynamics can make it difficult for teachers to give the time and energy that some children need. Some difficult children may be overtly defiant. The common scenario is that an adult makes a request. Children, rather than refusing to respond or comply, are noncompliant. Silence is their response—nonresponse. Or at best adults might get a guttural, "Huh? What?" Noncompliance often is effective to avoid directives or boundaries, especially when adults become distracted by other demands. Adults may also be hopeful that threats are sufficient to get children to behave as requested and they fail to monitor responses. If they don't actually follow through with consequences, children may continue to misbehave or not comply without suffering any repercussions. In other words, they get away with it. Successful noncompliance validates children's immature but strong drive to have power and control inappropriately. Children may initially not comply because of missing cues, distraction, inattention, processing issues, preoccupation, or purposeful testing of adults' frustration level. These are normal behaviors and do not predict problems if well handled by knowledgeable and skilled parents and, later, by teachers. However, when poorly handled, children's noncompliance eventually morphs into a loss of self-esteem and becomes purposefully aggressive. Parents or other adults ask and are ignored over and over and end up being controlled through noncompliance. Recognizing and validating children's strong desire for power and control is the first step in teaching appropriate avenues to gain them.

Parent Says and Does	Child Hears and Experiences
Oliver Daniel Duntz! You better turn off that TV and get to your room and do your homework!	Oliver Daniel Duntz! [huh?] Blah blah blah blah blah blah blah Blah blah blah blah blah blah blah blah blah blah blah blah!
One, two . . . *three!* [Eyes widen and nose flares]	One, two . . . *three!* [I'm watching TV!]
Oliver! That's it! [The parent jumps up, storms over to Oliver, and snatches him up by the arm]	*Oliver! That's it!* [What!? What's she doing!? Hey . . . hey! Watch out . . . Hey! Ow, my arm! *Ow! Ow! She's attacking me!*]
That's what you get for ignoring me!	*That's what you get for ignoring me!* [Whaaat!?]

Finally, adults can get so upset at continued misbehavior, noncompliance, or backtalk that they threaten, "If you don't . . . I'm going to . . . !" Adults may make increasingly severe threats but follow through erratically if at all, often with no or only mild consequences. Some parents never hit, but instead constantly emotionally and psychologically assault children. "What's wrong with you?" "I wish you were never born!" Even without damning words, the tone can be devastating. Frustrated teachers have their own versions of accusatory words. Children may internalize shame and learn a model of aggression. Eventually, some may respond with outrage, shouted out loud, or silently to themselves. The following statement can also apply to teachers or other adults besides parents.

Parents inadvertently reinforce child aggression by inadequately reinforcing pro-social behaviour. These parents do not model compliance and constructive problem solving. Instead, they support the aggressive and coercive behaviour of their children. Bullies, therefore, are likely to have primarily negative and hostile interactions with their siblings and parents. The second process relates to the harsh and inconsistent punishment practices of parents. Parents of bullies usually do not punish many problematic behaviours, and use overly harsh and punitive discipline with other behaviours. In so doing, parents model aggressive and antisocial problem-solving techniques. (Totten & Quigley, 2003, page 18)

In any communication, there is a verbal component and a nonverbal component. If the two components of communication are in sync with each other, then the entire message is perceived as being truthful. If the two components are at odds with each other, then the verbal message is normally dismissed as untrue and the nonverbal message believed to be true. Adults might verbally tell, direct, or command children to respond, but fail to follow through on implicit or explicit consequences. As a result, their verbalizations are dismissed. The lack of action, which is the nonverbal component, gives noncompliant children a contradictory message. They interpret adults' failure to act as if adults are not really asking them to respond! Ironically, as a result, children may experience subsequent appropriate adult discipline as unfair treatment! After so many times of getting away with it, actual discipline, no matter how reasonable, is unexpected and therefore "not fair!" "What!?" they say, while they are thinking, "So, why is it suddenly not OK to ignore you?" At this point, some adults who have lost control may respond very harshly and unpredictably. For example, parents of children with AS may express their frustration over their children's behavior with harsh treatment or discipline. Little (2003) says

rates of maternal verbal aggression (screaming and yelling, swearing, threatening to kick the child out, and calling the child names), were found to be higher than those reported by parents in a Gallup poll survey of children in the general population. . . . At the same time, rates of physical methods of discipline such as slapping, pinching and shaking the child, were also elevated. . . . In this study of 411 mothers of children with AS, mothers of ten year olds reported using verbal or psychological aggression the most (33 times a year), and mothers of four year olds with AS reported using spanking on the bottom with a hand or slapping the most (14 times in the last year). (p. 136)

Harsh parenting presents models of aggression that enforce children's feelings of helplessness and vulnerability, making many children vulnerable to bullying. Teachers may not know whether children have had other adults (parents or teachers) who have been consistent in their verbal and nonverbal communications. Some children have learned to count on teachers being distracted with other duties so that they can get away with noncompliance. It will take most teachers the first few days of school to discover which children are purposefully and consistently noncompliant. Only if teachers consistently monitor and follow through on their verbal communications with action to enforce compliance will such children learn that noncompliance is not acceptable.

If physical punishment has been experienced at home, it models physical aggression as appropriate responses to problems. Some frustrated adults blame children for the children getting punished. Adults may model intense self-righteous retaliatory anger that children may duplicate in their aggression against others. "I told you to stop!" "That's what you get for being so bad!" may be the responses of caring yet frustrated and unskilled caregivers. Punishment also can create resentment among children, prompting greater aggression against others. Antisocial behavior such as intentional physical harm is reinforced. Prosocial behaviors such as talking, exploring motivations and emotions, and affirming needs in the context of social reciprocal relationships, are not reinforced. Adults might be intimidated by anticipated disciplinary battles with children. Teachers are often caught between spending time and energy to resolve an issue and needing to attend to other issues, such as covering curriculum efficiently. As a result, adults may avoid confrontation by pulling back, failing to follow through, and letting children get away with misbehavior. At some level, children know that if they are in control and that adults are out of control, life is scary. Unable to articulate this fear, some children continue to be aggressive and hurtful. Immersed in their insecurity, bullies often don't or can't relate to or care about other people's feelings. Acknowledging others' feelings seems to negate the relevance of a bully's feelings. Admonishing bullies, "How would you like it if you were bullied . . ." is often completely ineffective. Bullies are usually unable to feel empathy or are so absorbed with their personal experiences that they don't consider others' feelings.

Teachers and parents need to stay calm when providing firm and reasonable boundaries and discipline. However, to do so, many adults need to address significant emotional, cultural, and psychological issues. In particular, teachers need to be aware of how they react to anger, conflict, and power and control issues intrinsic to difficult behaviors among children. Adults who do not address personal issues tend to be less effective with children's challenging behaviors. They also are more likely to be strongly and negatively activated by those behaviors. Sometimes, adults' personal issues may ignite or intensify children's already problematic behaviors. For example, if adults have control issues, having or working with children is sure to ignite them! Trying to control a classroom of children is more difficult than the metaphorical herding of cats. The cats don't talk back and cat herders don't have to teach mandated cat curriculum standards. Children can be directed and guided, but not controlled. Teachers can help children satisfy their needs for power and control only if they do not get drawn into power struggles with children. Personal growth about control needs becomes professional growth for such teachers. Teaching will always be about personal relationships amidst the curriculum, theories, strategies, and techniques. Teachers' personal relationships with children who are victimized and with children who bully others are vital to providing firm and reasonable discipline.

Chapter Highlights

- The desire to protect oneself and to deny further victimization should be considered strengths. This energy can be activated with appropriate guidance toward healthy self-empowerment.

- Unable to distinguish among socially acceptable assertiveness and bullying, bullies' behavior and reputation create misery for others and themselves for decades. From early on, bullies experience downward life spirals.

- Bullies' low self-esteem motivates their creation of a tenuous sense of worth based on aggression. Teachers can help such children gain self-esteem and, as a result, diminish their need to bully.

- Paranoia distorts bullies' perception and interpretation of innocent comments and behavior into believing that the other person was doing them "wrong."

- When poorly handled, children's noncompliance eventually morphs to loss of self-esteem and purposeful aggression against adults.

- Adults may model intense self-righteous retaliatory anger that children may duplicate in their aggression against others.

- Bullies experience acknowledgment of other people's feelings as conceding defeat in a feelings competition. Acknowledging others' feelings seems to negate the relevance of their own feelings.

- Teachers can help children satisfy their needs for power and control only if they do not get drawn into power struggles with children.

8

Relational Aggression

"YOU CAN'T COME TO MY BIRTHDAY PARTY"

At preschool, Kelli would gather her little covey of girls and purposefully exclude another girl. This girl could be wearing the wrong color, be the wrong color, be too smart, or have some other difference or challenge. People often focus on physical confrontations that are typical of male bullying, while minimizing female bullying. "You're not my best friend anymore!" However, many women remember painful childhood experiences without physical assault. "You can't come to my birthday party. You can't play with us." They may remember the experience of being bullied by other girls starting as early as preschool. "We don't like you ... we don't want to play with you!" It can continue through adolescence, often becoming most vicious in middle school or high school. "Come on girls. Let's go. There's something smelly here!"

Girls definitely can and do bully but may do so differently from boys. Male bullying tends to follow male social dynamics, which often is a struggle for status in the hierarchy. Being the "king of the hill," being or having the best or most, or being the alpha may be the primary goal for boys. Unless differences are honored, being different often sends one to the bottom, if allowed to stay in the hierarchy at all. In childhood, competitive physical aggression and domination usually establish male hierarchy. In arguably healthier male groups, a hierarchy is established that allows for some status for every member: an alpha, a beta, and lower ranked members. With ongoing struggles to maintain or ascend the hierarchy, everyone can have a more or less respected and valued place in the hierarchy. If low-status members show competence or make status-gaining progress, they can ascend the hierarchy. In the healthiest groups, all members value and celebrate the increased competence of any member.

Male bullies' self-esteem is based on destroying the self-esteem and power of others, rather than on showing greater personal competency relative to others. Aggressiveness or competitiveness to establish hierarchy in healthier male groups is distorted by bullies' need to destroy others. In normal hierarchies, bullies are at or near the bottom, that is, they're not well liked. Not respected or liked, bullies settle for being the most feared in a parallel social hierarchy. Competition for higher placement in the hierarchy becomes bullying for an illusion of power and control. Physical aggression expressed in games and sports becomes physical and hurtful exploitation, intimidation, and domination. "Winning" a game or race becomes an opportunity to destroy others emotionally and psychologically. Teachers can monitor these physical interactions, "rough housing," and playground games to see that assertion and aggression do not degenerate into abusive behavior. Left on their own in their physical play, boys may not hold themselves to appropriate boundaries. Children often experiment with what is or is not acceptable. When adults assert clear boundaries for them, it usually serves to stabilize the group. Children are more secure when they know and respect the boundaries and know that others will as well.

Ironically, the nonphysical aggression characteristic of girls may be indicative of developmental maturity. "Proponents of the stage theory of development argue that young children who lack verbal skills rely primarily on physical aggression. With the development of verbal and social skills, more sophisticated forms of aggression are possible" (Totten & Quigley, 2003, p. 15). Girls often are more socially conscious than are boys, resulting in distinctive female social dynamics or culture. Whereas hierarchy is foundational for male culture, inclusion in and exclusion from the group are often keys to female culture. Blachman and Hinshaw (2002) feel that status in the social domain is affected when girls have "male" characteristics of ADHD. He feels that girls who are more "boy-like" behaviorally don't do as well managing the female social standards among other girls.

> Evidence suggests that girls with ADHD suffer greater levels of peer rejection than their male counterparts. . . . In fact, although children with Inattentive-type ADHD (without hyperactivity) are often neglected (i.e., ignored) as opposed to rejected (i.e., actively disliked) by their peers, girls within this subtype are more rejected than boys. . . . In addition, the social interactions of girls, which tend to encompass smaller groups and focus on verbal interchanges . . . may place girls with ADHD at an added disadvantage because of the presence of cognitive and language deficits among

this group. . . . The increased risk for peer rejection among girls with ADHD, combined with the emphasis on dyadic or triadic close relationships among school-aged females . . . points to the importance of considering more closely the friendship patterns and experiences of this population. (p. 626)

Relationships among female members strongly determine social status, with intimacy as the greatest value. Sharing feelings becomes a way to bond (even in the supermarket checkout line with total strangers!). Being included within a female peer group becomes critical to emotional and psychological survival. Exclusion from the female peer group becomes tantamount to being emotionally abandoned in the wilderness. And historically those sent out from the community alone into the wilderness perished. Female bullying style often becomes about "relational aggression": hurting by damaging or manipulating relationships, spreading rumors to damage reputations, negative gossip, telling others to stop liking someone, withdrawal of friendship, social exclusion, and the silent treatment. These methods keep others in line, assert status, and build self-esteem for female bullies. "Femininity is related to dependence, nurturance, passivity, serving others, and maintenance of social relationships. Female aggression is contrary with the gender role expectations for girls. Consequently, they are more likely than boys to develop nonphysical forms of aggression for reasons related to social acceptability" (Totten & Quigley, 2003, p. 15).

To elude social disapproval, girls retreat beneath a surface of sweetness to hurt each other in secret. They pass covert looks and notes, manipulate quietly over time, corner one another in hallways, turn their back, whisper, and smile. The acts, which are intended to escape detection and punishment, are epidemic in middle-class environments where the rules of femininity are most rigid. (Simmons, 2002, p. 22)

One form in particular of Internet bullying, called "mean girls," is distinguished from other types of cyberbullying.

Typically, in the "Mean Girls" bullying situations, the cyberbullies are female. They may be bullying other girls (most frequently) or boys (less frequently). "Mean Girls" cyberbullying is usually done, or at least planned, in a group, either virtually or together in one room. This kind of cyberbullying is done for entertainment. It may occur from a school library or a slumber party, or from the family room of someone after school. This kind of cyberbullying requires an audience. The cyberbullies in a "mean girls" situation want others to know who they are and that they have the power to cyberbully others. This kind of cyberbullying grows when fed by group admiration, cliques or by the silence of others who stand by and let it happen. It quickly dies if they don't get the entertainment value they are seeking. (*What methods work*, 2008, Mean Girls section, ¶ 2)

The "entertainment" value or the reaction serves to feed cyberbullies. The Internet torture of fourteen-year-old Olivia Gardner persisted through two public schools into a private school (Lelchuk, 2007). Her classmates created an "Olivia Haters" Web page with postings calling her "homo," "bitch," and suggesting "kicking her ass." Taunting started in school when she had a seizure, resulting in classmates calling her a "retard." Although she switched schools, friends of students from her old school began harassing her within a week. Harassment followed her again despite moving again to a private school. In the cyber-community, bullying can be much more relentless than in a school community. There may be little or no escape. Parents and preschool teachers see relational bullying beginning as early as three or four years of age: "You're not my best friend." "You can't come to my birthday party." Little girls (and boys) are devastated. Unfortunately, some adults permit children's cruelty in choosing friends by overtly and loudly excluding others. They believe they cannot or should not tell children whom to choose as friends. However, teachers can require students to make friendship choices and still be socially responsibility and empathetic. They must stop those children who would intentionally hurt others. Adults need to intervene immediately to forbid harmful behavior and to administer appropriate consequences for cruelty.

WHAT DO YOU MEAN . . . "WE?"

People might think Kelli was a sweet little girl playing with the other girls. However, if they listened carefully, they would hear Kelli declare to her friends, "We don't like Joanie." The other girls, intimidated or otherwise under Kelli's influence, would probably go along. Kelli relished her domination of Joanie and the others. At four years old, Kelli was already quite the bully. Very sweet and charming to adults or when everything was going her way, she could turn vicious. Adult failure to intervene strongly and affirmatively would have been unconscionable.

I intervened. "Kelli, you are on time-out. You're trying to hurt Joanie's feelings on purpose. No one is allowed to hurt others on purpose at our school. Sit here." The basic rules of the community (family, class, school, society) are enforced. Children may be a part of the community only if they do not harm themselves, others, or the process of the community. Letting Kelli indulge in bullying Joanie and be rewarded with status or power portends her bullying others. To Kelli's gang, I challenged, "What did she mean . . . 'we'? You girls trying to be mean to Joanie too? Do you need to be on time-out too?"

> It is often said that one girl alone is rarely a problem, but get two or three together and they're different creatures entirely. Because girls often aggress as a group, exclusion and its cruel trappings can be a perversely good opportunity for secure companionship. An odd girl is out is undeniably so; her exclusion is made possible by the banding together of many. (Simmons, 2002, p. 134)

There was a quick chorus from the girls of, "Oh no! We like Joanie!!" I responded, "Oh you do? Then take Joanie and go play." "OK! Come on, Joanie . . . let's play!" And off they would go, leaving Kelli behind on time-out, *busted!* Adults must guarantee any social experimentation intimidating others to do cruel bidding turns out negatively for budding bullies. From a positive perspective, when the other girls were prompted to include Joanie, a new value and behavior of the group was created. The strong desire to be included in a group was still supported, but exclusion was tossed as a group value and behavior. Intervention for boys and girls is critical at the earliest ages. If a little girl like Joanie has difficulty responding to relational bullying, children with challenges may have even greater difficulty. For example, some children with AS may have hidden issues while in elementary school, but then find that hiding these issues in middle school is much more overwhelming. A *New York Times* article (Bazelon, 2007) quoted Catherine Lord, a veteran autism researcher:

> "The girls often have the potential to really develop relation-ships . . . But by middle school, a subset of them is literally dumb-struck by anxiety. They do things like bursting into tears or lashing out in school, which make them very conspicuous. Their behavior really doesn't jibe with what's expected of girls. And that makes their lives very hard." (p. 2)

Bazelon notes the rising level of social interaction compared to earlier years that comes in middle school.

> Girls' networks become intricate and demanding, and friendships often hinge on attention to feelings and lots of rapid and nuanced communication. . . . No matter how much they want to connect, autistic girls are not good at empathy and conversation, and they find themselves locked out, seemingly even more than boys do. (p. 2)

It becomes increasingly difficult to intervene against relational bullying in preadolescence and adolescence as social dynamics evolve. Relational bullying in early childhood may be clumsy and problematic and readily observed by adults. However, in later years, it can become calculating and conducted under the adult supervision umbrella. Thunfors (2005), in his study of 379 middle school students, found that "Instead of suffering social repercussions for the maltreatment of their peers, the majority of bullies were either high or medium in their peer popularity status" (Conclusions section, ¶ 1). This was particularly true for girl bullies (50%; 7 of 14). "Although bullying is disapproved of, it is a way to assert social dominance and we speculate that it may serve to *facilitate* the attainment of popularity among early adolescent peers" (Conclusions section, ¶ 1). A study of 1,756 middle school children in Korea that found that students of high social economic status (SES) were more likely to be perpetrators of bullying, while those of both high and low SES are more likely to be victims (Kim, Koh, & Levanthal, 2004). Students of higher SES easily victimized more vulnerable lower SES students, while also victimizing other students of high SES to maintain popularity among peers.

Bullying really works for these students! No wonder so many teen movie plots (*Mean Girls*, Waters, 2004; *The Breakfast Club*, Hughes, 1985; *The Karate Kid*, Avildsen, 1984, *Carrie*, De Palma, 1976) revolve around popular kids tormenting one or more classmates. This socially toxic form of gaining dominance and popularity bodes increasingly greater harm as children get older. The desire to be popular among classmates is normal. It needs to be guided so that it is acquired in socially healthy ways, without harming others' self-esteem. Teachers often find that the bullies of high school were practicing bullies in middle school. Many times, their former kindergarten and early elementary teachers are not surprised to hear they are still bullies. Bullying personas, skills, and strategies can start early. School and districtwide processes need to be implemented to direct children to healthier strategies to gain popularity, power, and control. Without adamant and relentless adult intervention, the culture of classrooms and playgrounds can evolve to tolerate and then condone bullying behavior as a means to social status. The institutional culture of verbalized condemnation but functional tolerance and permission for bullying behavior in schools can only be changed through institutionalizing greater adult vigilance and supervision. Increased supervision cannot just be a matter of vigilance. Teachers are already inundated with work demands. Increased supervision requires additional human power in terms of staffing and improved training of supervisors as well as a financial commitment. The standards movement has institutionalized heightened accountability for academic achievement and, in some cases, increased resources. Teachers and other concerned adults need to demand that schools institutionalize heightened accountability for children's social and emotional safety as well.

Chapter Highlights

- Aggressiveness or competitiveness to establish hierarchy in healthier male groups is distorted by bullies' need to destroy others.

- Whereas hierarchy is foundational for male culture, inclusion in and, subsequently, exclusion from the group are often keys to female culture.

- Female bullying style often becomes about "relational aggression": hurting by damaging or manipulating relationships, spreading rumors to damage reputations, negative gossip, telling others to stop liking someone, withdrawal of friendship, social exclusion, and the silent treatment.

- Teachers can require individuals to make friendship choices and still be socially responsibility and empathetic. They must stop those children who would intentionally hurt others and who ensure that excluded people feel ostracized and isolated without recourse.

- Adults must guarantee that any social experimentation in intimidation of others to do cruel bidding turns out negatively for budding bullies.

- Students of higher social economic status (SES) easily victimized more vulnerable lower SES students, while also victimizing other students of high SES to maintain popularity among peers.

- The institutional culture of verbalized condemnation but functional tolerance and permission for bullying behavior in schools can only be changed through institutionalizing greater adult vigilance and supervision.

9

Frustration to Resentment to Aggression

LOST SELF-ESTEEM

When children's challenges cause frustration and failure, it leads to both functional and dysfunctional attempts to reassert lost self-esteem and power. Functional responses may be developed intuitively depending on children's social-emotional intelligence, counterbalancing strengths from the challenges, or children's natural personalities or aptitudes. Functional responses are more likely than not to be fostered through adult guidance. For example, adults may direct children to their physical strengths and encourage them to get involved in sports or dance. Enriching the curriculum through differentiated instruction for gifted children helps them explore their interests. Establishing a quiet and more isolated spot for distractible children to read not only helps them be more successful, but also teaches them a successful compensation. One teacher organized a classroom club based on an activity that a child who had trouble developing social relationships knew a lot about. The child was able to shine as an expert in the club. Without adult guidance, children with challenges can easily gravitate to dysfunctional or disruptive responses. Teachers may identify behaviors as problematic but not realize that they may be a result of children's loss of self-esteem. If they respond with boundaries, consequences, or other discipline, these adults inadvertently further frustrate such children instead of offering support or guidance. Can you match the challenge or frustration with the typical response teachers might see in their classroom or playground?

Challenge or Frustration	Response
Has trouble reading because of a learning disability . . .	and then gets mad at them!
Gets into trouble for not sitting still or keeping hands to self . . .	and then is hurt they don't like her.
Can be so relentless and articulate telling other kids they're wrong . . .	and hides embarrassment by bugging others.
Goes on and on even when others aren't interested, annoying them . . .	and terrorizes the playground with his gang.

Adapting to school demands is a formative experience for children as they develop skills for successful adult functioning. Depending on individual characteristics or challenges, children are more or less prepared or encumbered to handle stressful integration into school. Without guidance, they often find other ways to gain some semblance of self-esteem, status, or power. Seeking power and control, often to mask inferiority, can lead to tactics such as bullying. The bullying behavior makes them social outcasts, compromises learning, and repels otherwise supportive adults. Teachers can learn to recognize typical behavioral responses that are often characteristic of particular challenges. These include choices that can lead to bullying others in their communities, in the classroom, playground, and later in life.

A specific challenge or frustration does not automatically or consistently draw any particular response, positive or negative. Trouble reading because of an LD may result in a child seeking assistance reading rather than seeking power and control through intimidating others. Criticized for inability to sit still, another child may use her energy and find productive ways to be active through sports. Or children may adapt their behavior to better get along with others. No specific response should be considered absolutely indicative of any particular challenge. However, observant teachers can often recognize typical unsuccessful responses. They can infer common potential causes, which in turn can activate prudent exploration of what might be frustrating children. Bullying behavior may be the consequence directly or indirectly of identifiable challenges that teachers can help children resolve.

BULLIES WITH LEARNING DISABILITIES

Challenges of children with LD can result in classroom problems, resentment, and aggression against both innocents and those culpable of aggression against them. An LD does not make children act out. However, if children with LD are not well supported, their frustration can lead to acting out behavior. For example, Alan has an LD that causes him to be not as efficient as others retrieving information from his memory. As a result, he needs more time to find or figure out answers to questions. Alan can cite many experiences from spontaneous memory, but his on-demand memory recall (also known as involuntary versus voluntary memory) is inefficient. Conscious effort in remembering events, people, and places is required when the teacher asks, "What is the king of the jungle and roars loudly?" Children with efficient on-demand memory recall snatch the answer quickly from their memory storage and call out, "Lion!" Alan, on the other hand, searches his on-demand memory storage room for the answer. This storage room has several file cabinets of knowledge. "Which file cabinet? Not the plant cabinet. Not the book or television storage cabinet. OK . . . animals' cabinet. Which drawer in the animals' cabinet? Hmmm? Drawers for the wild . . . the domesticated . . . the aquatic animals . . . Yes, the wild land animal drawer at the top. Hmmm . . . a bunch of folders for different continents and for predators versus prey animals." Finally, leafing through the African predator folder, Alan discovers the answer.

Excitedly, Alan starts to call out the answer. Unbeknownst to him, other children have already answered the question with "Lion!" And the teacher has already asked a new question, "What is tall and has a long neck and eats from the top of trees?" Before the other children can shout, "Giraffe!" Alan calls out, "Lion!" There is a moment of shocked silence . . . then hilarious laughter. The kids think he's really funny! The teacher thinks it's a bit funny this time. After the second and third time, the teacher doesn't think it's funny anymore, and scolds Alan, "Stop being a wise guy!" Eventually, his classmates get annoyed at the distracting behavior and copy the teacher's model of annoyance. Alan ends up getting teased, then later ostracized, and eventually bullied by classmates. Alan, despite trying so hard to please the teacher and to keep up, finds he cannot be successful at either. Labeled a clown or stupid by classmates and punished by everyone for trying, Alan becomes sullen and resentful, a silent seething tantrum. Repeated failures from diagnosed and undiagnosed LD can foster great frustration, loss of self-esteem, and resentment. Resentment initially may be directed at adults. However, since adults are too powerful to act against, they may slide deeper into silent anxiety, depression, and anger. Norwich and Kelly (2004), in a study of 101 bullied British students with moderate LD found deep wells of hidden rage in some children.

> "Well, I generally feel very angry . . . and there are times where I get so angry and I'll just bottle it up and I just want to walk behind them and hit them in the head . . . that is what happened at my old school, I ended up hurting someone who was not anything to do with the problem . . . who just happened to get in the way accidentally." (p. 57)

Aggression against others may be experienced as justified retaliation for the covert and overt verbal, social, and physical attacks or exclusions. Children who cannot build themselves up or ascend the classroom or playground hierarchy through academic or social competence may resort to taking others down. By bullying other children, children with LD such as Alan "raise" themselves in the social hierarchy. Johnson (2002) found in a survey of research a significant association between LD and behavior problems, both internalizing behaviors (withdrawal, anxiety, depression, phobias, somatic problems, feelings of intellectual inadequacy) and externalizing behaviors (defiance, impulsivity, hyperactivity, aggression, and antisocial features). Children suffer emotional and psychological damages that may not be discernible to teachers. They may not get much if any support with the internal damages as a result. On the other hand, their externalizing behaviors are readily noted, and discipline tends to follow. Children with challenges are sometimes unable to build socially reciprocating relationships (based on affection and respect) because of their behaviors. Such friendships would potentially assuage their unseen internal damages. Aggressive social behaviors such as intimidation can become the only avenues to any substantial social relationship, however dysfunctional. Teacher empathy or support for their LD may fade as bullying behavior begins to dominate. Social isolation develops. When children bully or otherwise act out, teachers should assess for potential LD that may be at the core of their misbehavior. When children are diagnosed as having an LD, teachers need to monitor whether academic or social challenges will lead to frustration that precipitate problematic behavior.

BULLIES WITH ADHD

Since ADHD can be considered a type of LD, children with ADHD and children with LD share many academic, emotional, and social consequences. The core symptoms of ADHD (hyperactivity, impulsivity, and inattention) create difficulties with self-awareness and self-regulation that often cause problems with self-control in social and academic interactions. Hyperactivity expressed as greater physicality in both supervised and unsupervised situations leads to more bumps and bruises not only for children with ADHD but also for their playmates. Leaping before looking due to impulsivity, children with ADHD may seize the moment. Even if they remember previous incidents, some children have trouble adjusting their impulsive energy. Satisfying the immediate impulse becomes the only relevant or most compelling motivation. They become more likely to crash themselves and classmates into physical and social crises. Classmates eventually blame them for getting them into trouble. As Oliver Hardy says to Stan Laurel (Parrot, 1930), "Well, here's another nice mess you've gotten me into!" in the movie *Another Fine Mess*. Like Stan Laurel, children with ADHD may get berated or even smacked shortly thereafter. Adults often lose patience when children do not self-regulate energy to adult expectations. Peers intuit adult impatience and may assume teachers condone negative judgment and reputations. Sonji (2008) described what happened to her son with ADHD:

I remember when the reports started piling in from my son's kindergarten class that he was hitting children in school. Some kids were saying he was pushing them, kicking them and even biting them. I didn't believe it. None of these stories made sense to me because it was behavior that we had never seen at home. To us he was a very kind, jovial, and happy child who was energetic and full of life. But to the students and teachers at school, my son was a troublemaker, a clown and a distraction to everyone in his class.

While visiting the school, I noticed that every move my son made was closely monitored by the other students. If he accidentally bumped into someone he was reported for hitting. If he dropped something, he was charged with throwing things. If he spoke to someone too closely he was called a "spitter."

No matter what my son did, he was doing it wrong in the eyes of others. And many times when he was accused of bad things he fought back, sometimes very hard like a bully. His interaction with others was so all over the place I couldn't tell if my son was a victim of the negative reports, or truly a bully as reported.

Children don't need a lot of negative experiences to begin disliking others.

Many have noted that it takes few social exchanges over a period of only 20–30 minutes between children with ADHD and nondisabled children for the latter children to find the former disruptive, unpredictable, and aggressive, and hence to react to them with aversion, criticism, rejection, and sometimes even counter-aggression. (Barkley, 2006, pp. 199–200)

Blachman and Hinshaw (2002) in their survey of research found that

children with ADHD have been repeatedly found to experience extremely high rates of peer rejection—presumably as a result of their intrusive and disruptive behaviors, limited understanding of the impact of their behavior on others, and strong likelihood of comorbid oppositionality or aggression. . . . Such peer rejection occurs almost immediately upon social contact . . . and even those children with ADHD who are not aggressive tend to be rejected because of their overzealous and insensitive behaviors. . . . Children with ADHD often serve as "negative social catalysts," fueling conflictual social interactions among their peers. (¶ 2)

Children's impulsivity precludes careful consideration of all potential factors in decision making. They have trouble considering other people's thoughts, feelings, and needs, and anything other than short-term gratification. Inattention causes them to miss important social cues. Classmates experience their feelings and needs ignored or bowled over. This happens despite children with ADHD's honest assertion that they were not ignoring them or trying to hurt them. Distracted and impulsive children cannot ignore what they did not notice in the first place! Teachers need to not just admonish such children to look before they leap, but to anticipate the situations that require consideration before action. Adults often complain, "This kid does this all the time!" Children with high impulsivity are actually very predictable. If something is new or attractive or there is an immediate short-term benefit, a whole lotta leap'n is gonna happen! Adults need to identify the new, attractive situations that offer such children immediate short-term benefits. Then, before they happen, they can direct the leapers to look carefully and consider long-term consequences before acting. "Going out is going to be really exciting, so think about how you're going to act." "Everyone will want it first; remember, anyone (meaningful look to child right about now!) who pushes or grabs won't get a turn." Next, adults should not assume that the warnings, which are a form of focusing children with impulsivity, will work by themselves. Teachers also need to monitor children as they move into any tempting situation and immediately focus or direct them as needed. The teacher should validate them for their "success" in resisting their impulsivity. Managing impulsivity is critical to social success. Children's impulsivity when merged with or interpreted as aggressive behavior moves them closer to either becoming bullies or being perceived by others as being bullies.

People with ADHD may express symptoms of aggression or anger or have emotional outbursts. Gagnon, Craig, Tremblay, Zhou, & Vitaro (1995) suggest that while aggression does not predict hyperactivity, there is a relationship between early hyperactivity and aggressive behavior problems. It is arguable whether aggression is a function of the ADHD condition or a response to academic, emotional, and social frustration from ADHD symptoms. A study by Finnish researchers found in both teacher and parent ratings for both genders substantial intercorrelations between aggression and hyperactivity-impulsivity. They found "that both genetic and environmental factors are important in creating the correlation between aggression and hyperactivity-impulsivity" (Vierikko, Pulkkinen, Kaprio, & Rose, 2004, p. 270). The correlation may exist because environmental influences may be elicited by the genetic influence of hyperactivity-impulsivity. In other words, the energy and traits of ADHD expressed behaviorally will draw responses (for example, anger, rejection, aggression, etc.) from others that will amplify the ADHD energy and traits. If so, parental and teacher discipline with children with ADHD also has substantial potential to prevent and ameliorate negative consequences such as aggression.

Bullying for some children with ADHD becomes a response to regain self-worth, power, and control. Social status is thus based on dominating and intimidating others as opposed to gaining their affection or respect. Holmberg and Hjern (2007) studied an entire population of 577 fourth graders (ten-year-olds) in one municipality in Stockholm, Sweden. They confirmed a common assertion that children with ADHD are both more likely to be bullies (four times more likely) and also more likely to be victims of bullies (ten times more likely!). Another study using a sample of 1315 middle school students found that children with ADHD were more likely than control students to be targeted to be victimized by bullies (34% to 22%), but also were more likely than other children to bully others (13% to 8%) (Unnever & Cornell, 2003). Classmates who suffer the consequences of ADHD distractibility, impulsivity, or hyperactivity usually do not distinguish between bullying and unintended harmful behavior. Children with ADHD may resent being mislabeled as bullies or callously aggressive, especially by frustrated adults. Children who suffer intensifying despair, deteriorating self-esteem, and resentment from feeling misunderstood and isolated may become unreceptive to adult support. Distinguishing between bullying and behaviors influenced by ADHD and other conditions is vital to intervention. The relationship of ADHD to other childhood disruptive disorders shows correlations that imply potential but not necessarily causal relationships. Here are definitions of two more severe diagnoses: oppositional defiant disorder and conduct disorder.

Oppositional defiant disorder (ODD) is characterized among other criteria "by a recurrent pattern of negativistic, defiant, disobedient and hostile behavior toward authority figures" (American Psychiatric Association, 1994, p. 91).

Conduct disorder (CD) is characterized among other criteria by

> repetitive and persistent pattern of behavior in which the basic rights of others or major age-appropriate societal norms or rules are violated . . . four main groupings: aggressive conduct that causes or threatens physical harm to other people or animals . . . , nonaggressive conduct that causes property loss or damage . . . , deceitfulness or theft, and serious violations of rules. (p. 85)

The symptoms of the three disruptive behavior disorders (ADHD, ODD, and CD) show substantial evidence of overlap across dimensions, with very important distinctions. ODD behavior is intentionally defiant and negative toward authority figures, but not normally toward classmates. In comparison, ADHD behavior often affects everyone but is not necessarily targeted in opposition toward anyone. ADHD behavior comes primarily from internal energy that does not necessarily require another's reaction. ADHD behavior may be functionally but innocently aggressive, while ODD behavior is purposefully aggressive and meant to inflict harm. CD involves the explicit disregard of others' rights and community standards to serve personal gratification. In fact, the personal gratification of someone with CD occurs primarily from violating others' rights and community standards. ADHD behavior is not gratifying to children with

ADHD. Quite the opposite—they ordinarily are quite remorseful for the harm they cause. They care, rather than not care, about others and the community. If misunderstood and pathologized, children with ADHD may develop ODD or CD. Distinctions among these diagnoses are critical to learn. Without realizing it, teachers may be substituting in lay terminology code words such as "wild children" for ADHD, "negative children" for ODD, or "cruel kids" for CD.

Teachers are the professionals most intimately involved with children. They, more than other professionals, need to be aware of cultural presumptions that distinguish disruptive disorders. Bias and prejudice may affect diagnosis and subsequent treatment or interactions. Teacher perspectives, including unconscious bias, may cause overdiagnosis of LD and ADHD for minority children. The three-year study by Harry and Klingner (2007) on the special education placement process for black and Hispanic students in a large urban school district found a disproportionate placement of blacks and Hispanics with an LD label. This study reversed an earlier historical trend of the diagnosis being given to mainly white and middle-class students. Diagnosis is intended to activate support. However, if it becomes misdiagnosis, it has the opposite effect of causing exclusion from services or maltreatment with inappropriate services. There are many potential socioeconomic status explanations for the diagnostic differences—prejudice, economic status, educational status, family composition, and so forth—that need to be taken into consideration to prevent a diagnosis from becoming harmful. McNeil, Cappage, and Bennett (2002) believe culturally bound behaviors may be confused with psychopathology and that professionals often lack training to counter cultural bias (p. 339). Socioeconomic status, parental stress, and family constellation have been identified as correlates for disruptive child behaviors and vary among different cultural groups. McNeil et al. cited numerous studies with differential professional diagnosis by race. One study found Caucasian children more likely to be diagnosed with ODD, while African-American children were more likely to be diagnosed with the more severe diagnosis of CD. Minorities, boys, and low-income children are more likely to be diagnosed with persistent serious problems relating to neurological, attention, and conduct functioning. Symptoms (including hallucinations, paranoid thought patterns, bizarre behaviors such as swallowing sharp objects) exhibited by Caucasian children that would be viewed as problematic were sometimes overlooked with black children (p. 345). Responsible professionals need to be vigilant against any potential bias incorrectly assuming relationships between certain populations and certain diagnoses. In addition, care should be taken not to overstate relationships among diagnoses. When studies find correlations among ADHD, ODD, and CD, it creates fear of a relationship between ADHD and later substance abuse, domestic violence, and criminality, including sexual assault (Maryland Institute Research Reports, n.d.). The fear can harm children, whether such relationships are based on reality, misinterpretation, or bias. Accurate unbiased assessment helps teachers make sound interventions and provide appropriate support to prevent inaccurately stigmatizing children. Accurate diagnosis leading to effective intervention also helps to preclude potential progression from ADHD issues to ODD, CD, bullying, and other destructive life practices.

Chapter Highlights

- Seeking power and control, often to mask inferiority, can lead to tactics such as bullying. The bullying behavior makes such children social outcasts, compromises learning, and repels otherwise supportive adults.

- Repeated failures from diagnosed and undiagnosed learning disabilities can foster great frustration, self-esteem loss, and resentment.

- Whenever children bully others or otherwise act out, teachers need to assess for potential learning disabilities that may be at the core of their misbehavior. And whenever children are diagnosed as potentially having a learning disability, teachers need to monitor whether academic or social challenges will lead to frustration that precipitates problematic behavior.

- The core symptoms of ADHD (hyperactivity, impulsivity, and inattention) create difficulty with self-awareness and self-regulation that often causes problems with self-control in social and academic interactions.

- Children don't need a lot of negative experiences to begin disliking others.

- Classmates who suffer the consequences of ADHD distractibility, impulsivity, or hyperactivity usually do not distinguish between bullying and unintended harmful behavior.

- People may incorrectly lump ADHD behavioral characteristics automatically with ODD intentions against others and conduct disorder amorality.

- Diagnosis is intended to activate support. However, if it becomes misdiagnosis, it has the opposite effect of causing exclusion from services or maltreatment with inappropriate services.

10

Arrogance and Entitlement

BULLIES WITH ASPERGER SYNDROME

The saying goes "Power corrupts. . . ." The traditional bully usually has some kind of physical superiority over his victim. If not size then the knowledge or skill to hurt someone physically. People with Asperger Syndrome are superior usually in the IQ department. Therefore, when they bully, it's more like psychological bullying. I know because I have Asperger's and I've done it before. It's not something that I intended to do, it just escalated from nothing to full blown bullying. I backed down when I realized what I was doing. I was bullied in school by traditional bullies. Maybe it rubbed off on me.

This answer to the question "Can people with Asperger syndrome bully?" was posted on the Web site uk.answers.yahoo.com (2008). The responses above and following were either first-person admissions of bullying by individuals with AS or direct observations, including by relatives bullied by individuals with AS. A sense of superiority is often a common trait of the individuals who bully.

Most certainly. My brother has it and he can bully if he doesn't keep close tabs on himself. And he's a pastor. He's gotten much better. Strangely enough, he's always backed down very fast. He's easy to shut down. He is sensitive and can be hurt easily.

My nephew has this condition and yes he bullies . . . but generally people a lot younger than him. I guess he feels "superior." . . . He doesn't see he is doing wrong as that's the way the condition makes him. . . . He does fly off the handle and has become violent at times but again it is the condition and how it affects him. He sees he is doing "normal" things that generally are not acceptable to those not having the condition.

Bauer (1996) notes that AS shows a range of symptom severity. This means some children may meet criteria but not get diagnosed. They seem a bit unusual, different, or may be misdiagnosed with ADHD and emotional disturbance. Children with AS may laugh or giggle when others show embarrassment, discomfort, or sadness. Adults and peers often misinterpret this response of children with AS as mocking or otherwise disrespecting their feelings or thoughts. Children with AS often have difficulty conveying disturbance, anxiety, or distress. Sometimes they have delayed reactions stemming from events that occurred much earlier.

The child may worry about something, not communicate his or her feelings to parents and eventually, perhaps hours or days later, release the build up of emotions in a "volcanic" emotional explosion. Such children keep their thoughts to themselves and replay an event in their thoughts to try to understand what happened. Each mental action replay causes the release of the associated emotions and eventually the child can cope no longer. The frustration, fear, or confusion has reached an intensity that is expressed by very agitated behavior. (Attwood, 2006, p. 132)

Others ascribe, often incorrectly, children's unexpected or agitated behavior to an assortment of causes. Kiriana Cowansage was not diagnosed with AS until she was nineteen. Throughout childhood, she handled teasing and harassment poorly and became confused about social interactions.

The boys would provoke her—say, by stealing her pencils. Over time, she began to suspect that any time a boy spoke to her it was to mock her. She became defensively standoffish. "I just wanted them not to talk to me, so I pulled together as much blunt sarcasm as I could and established myself as a weird, unfriendly girl." (Flora, 2006, p. 99)

It worked. Despite being relatively attractive, at twenty-four years old, she has never had a boyfriend. Although she was seen as strange with odd interests and behaviors as a child, adults never diagnosed her with AS. They merely thought she was a negative person.

Aggressive behavior may be reactive to being bullied in combination with a sense of superiority that can develop among children with AS. This type of bullying is similar to the "vengeful angel" described on the Web site stopcyberbullying.org. These bullies are distinguished from "power-hungry" cyberbullies, who are basically similar to playground bullies. Classic playground bullies exert their authority and show that they are powerful over others. Or they use fear effectively to make others do what they want. Vengeful bullies, however, don't

> see themselves as bullies at all. They see themselves as righting wrongs, or protecting themselves or others from the "bad guy" they are now victimizing. This includes situations when the victim of cyberbullying or offline bullying retaliates and becomes a cyber-bully themselves. They may be angry at something the victim did and feel they are taking warranted revenge or teaching the other a lesson. (*What methods work*, "Vengeful Angel" section, ¶ 1)

Children with AS may be particularly prone to self-righteous vengeance because they often feel victimized for no reason they can discern. They may have done something or several things that have been disturbing or hurtful to others, but do not realize it due to misreading social cues from offended parties. Connor (1999) discusses how some characteristics of AS result in behavior not intended to be aggressive that nevertheless may look aggressive to others:

> Children and young people diagnosed with this syndrome are not inherently prone to aggression or violence. However, the social dif-ficulties may often lead to anxiety or frustration or stress which, in turn, can lead to behaviour which appears aggressive. Converging evidence has shown that what might seem to be aggressive behav-iour is actually motivated by a need to escape from a stressful situation . . . the person may appear odd or even provocative, and other young people may be irritated by some of these behaviours, such as an unwillingness to take turns, a misunderstanding of social rules, agitation if his/her space is encroached upon, and the appar-ent self-centredness . . . a kind of vicious circle is set up whereby the young person becomes increasingly set apart, continues to have dif-ficulty in expressing how (s)he feels, and develops greater feelings of stress linked to what appears to be a lack of control over uncom-fortable situations, until a crisis point is reached. . . . The feelings of stress and loss of control may result in behaviours which appear aggressive but which, in fact, reflect the difficulty in functioning in a world seen to be unpredictable. (Connor, 1999, Aggression and Asperger Syndrome section, ¶ 3, 5, 6)

The offended parties may retaliate for what they perceive as purposeful attacks. Then children with AS will experience the retaliation as com-pletely unjustified attacks. This motivates them to strike back, often verbally. "I retaliated righteously, they sneak attacked!" A mutually retaliatory and intensifying cycle of aggression then ensues.

By middle school, Chester had a long history of increasingly aggressive behaviors and altercations. He was often arrogant and defiant with teachers and his mother. He frequently threatened classmates with graphic descriptions of violence against them. Difficulties reading social cues make children like Chester seem odd to others. Supportive adults in preschool and elementary years tend to be more effective at enforcing inclusion and tolerance with young children such as Chester. Adult management enforcing peer acceptance gradually may break down in later grades as teachers' priorities shift from socialization to curriculum demands. The shift from single teacher and classroom in elementary school to multiple teachers and classrooms in middle school further dilutes adult management. Initially, classmates found Chester difficult to deal with. As he grew older, classmates often didn't like him, sometimes teased him, and either frequently avoided or excluded him. Some classmates were more aggressive and hurtful. Some children with AS, naive about children with cruel intentions and about social interactions, are easily manipulated. Highly judgmental but insecure preteens, wanting to boost their fragile senses of self-esteem, may ridicule children with AS for any oddities or missteps.

> Kids with AS were four times more likely to be bullied, twice as likely to be hit or kicked in their privates, and twice as likely to be hit by peers and siblings . . . also . . . children with AS and NLD experience high levels of peer shunning that seem to increase with age and peak in high school. Middle school is a time when most children are trying to fit in and not be noticed as being "different." Also, middle and high school are times when peers are more important and peer pressure influences much of what is considered "socially appropriate behavior." Because children with AS stand out and are alone more often than their typical peers, they are at greater risk for bullying and shunning at a time when peer acceptance is most critical. (Heinrichs & Myles, 2003, p. 7)

Normal but difficult preadolescent and adolescent developmental emotional, psychological, social, and cultural storms are challenging. Accumulated social and emotional damages from negative treatment from peers and adults due to undiagnosed and unsupported AS behaviors can become explosive in middle school. Socially isolated and feeling vulnerable to others' aggression, Chester decided that he needed to present himself as dangerous to others. Eventually, classmates became scared as he escalated threats of retaliation for offenses he felt they had committed against him. He boasted that he could and would hurt anyone that did him wrong. This attitude is similar to what on the Web site stopcyberbullying.org is called "inadvertent cyberbullies," who

> usually don't think they are cyberbullies at all. They may be pretending to be tough online, or role playing, or they may be reacting to hateful or provocative messages they have received . . . they don't lash out intentionally. They just respond without thinking about the consequences of their actions. They may feel hurt, or angry because of a communication sent to them, or something they have seen online. And they tend to respond in anger or frustration. (*What methods work,* Inadvertent Cyberbully section, ¶ 1–2)

It seemed Chester was obsessed with violence. This was not surprising considering he had witnessed domestic violence by his stepfather against his mother. His stepfather asserted a "tough" persona and modeled emotionally and physically aggressive behaviors. His stepfather had been reported to authorities for unreasonably severe corporal punishment constituting physical child abuse inflicted on Chester and his younger brother. Chester often bragged how tough he was, although he had never been an actual physical fight.

Chester had more problems when there was a complexity of social cues that he needed to interpret. He had trouble distinguishing the meanings among different facial expressions and voice tones as happy, sad, upset, or something else. He gave few nonverbal facial and postural cues to others to indicate that he understood, agreed with, or integrated what other people were communicating. He appeared indifferent to them. Perhaps he thought he looked cool. This flat affect was deceptive because as Connor (1999) notes, "An appearance of particular detachment or calm may actually reflect stress; and a major goal for teachers or parents is to recognise when the stress is being generated thus to alter the situation before the stress becomes critical" (Aggression and Asperger Syndrome section, ¶ 15). Unfortunately, adults did not recognize how the accumulation of stress both from his underlying issues and from his family and school environments expressed in his behavior.

In addition to his family dynamics, AS was a major underlying issue. Chester was unable to recognize subtle social cues from others that gave feedback that his behavior was intrusive or annoying. In early childhood, Chester was completely surprised and hurt as people rejected him. Resentments morphed into a kind of paranoia that others were out to harm him. He felt entitled to avenge actual and perceived injustices. Some of his victims were children that had harmed him, but others were targeted because he could dominate them. Early recognition of the multiple factors leading to this behavior and attitudes could have directed intervention and precluded his becoming a misfit, rejection by classmates, and misunderstanding by teachers. Early family dynamics and the failure of accurate professional assessment, awareness, and support allowed negative attitudes and paranoid perspectives to become firmly entrenched. Subsequent attempts at making intervention became much more difficult. The following two comments on the Web site uk.answers.yahoo.com to the question about whether children with Asperger syndrome can bully point to innocent origins of negative behavior.

> I know someone with Aspergers Syndrome and I would say yes. But I don't think they even know they are doing it and don't see it as wrong. The person I know has very little empathy and doesn't realize when they are hurting your feelings—to him, it's perfectly reasonable to say the things he does.

> I think that people with Aspergers Syndrome can not bully as such but can be in a way mean towards people. Because of their unliked and unwanted communication with others they are likely to not want to torment/bully people. Although they can say some strange things at times which can cause offense.

Children with AS may not be fully aware of their increasing emotional stress and deterioration in mood over time. They may become too overwhelmed for thoughtful control. One reaction to realization of being different is to become arrogant, with intolerant standards and expectations of others. Since being different often has an implicit negative stigma, some children may reverse the negativity to label the nondifferent children as inferior. People who don't measure up to them are seen as stupid or deliberately trying to confuse or annoy them. Tending to feel very angry when confused or frustrated, they think of retribution, destruction, punishment and physical retaliation (Attwood, 2006, p. 145). Haskins and Silva (2006) researched the components of AS or high functioning autistic spectrum disorders (hfASD) that might increase vulnerability to breaking the law. They make clear that having a developmental disorder does not necessarily enhance the likelihood of acting criminally. Rather, they described the features of hfASD that would most likely be involved when criminal actions occur.

> Criminal activity associated with hfASD psychopathology can be divided into two broad domains: (1) deficits in Theory of Mind (ToM) abilities and/or (2) abnormal, repetitive narrow interests. Theory of Mind (or mentalization) refers to the ability to estimate the cognitive, perceptual, and affective life of others as well as of the self. This relative inability to utilize ToM abilities has been termed "mindblindness." HfASD individuals have substantial difficulties with reading social cues. HfASD perpetrators generally present with significant deficits in their abilities to know that another person has a different emotional cognitive experience of a

shared event. They may suffer from an inability to read the necessary interpersonal cues telling the perpetrator to disengage from a social encounter. (p. 378)

They conclude with preliminary findings that indicate that people with hfASD are over-represented in the criminal populations relative to their prevalence in the general population. They make additional recommendations for further research into empathy, remorse, risk factors for psychopathology, impulsivity, and ToM characteristics of hfASDs. Katz and Zemishlany (2006), from their work in Israel, basically concur:

> AS . . . criminal behavior . . . may result from a change in routine or from running into a social situation which people with AS are unable to understand and, therefore, perceive as threatening. They display intense preoccupation with their special areas of interest and may react violently when disturbed or prevented from doing something related to these interests. They lack empathy and the ability to associate actions with their results. (p. 166)

Intense reactions, aggressive behavior, bullying, and possible criminality may all be linked through the core vulnerabilities created by the syndrome. "They may be highly provoked by noise, and sometimes, in an attempt to be liked by others, they may be persuaded by these others to commit thefts, physical and sexual assaults, etc." (p. 166). Potential criminality as a result of poorly addressed AS in childhood (or other challenges) may sound unreasonably foreboding. Caution needs to be taken not to equate AS, or any other challenge that is believed to have a statistically higher-than-expected relationship with a negative outcome, with a definitive causal relationship. On the other hand, teachers and parents need to recognize that children's problematic behavior that violates classmates' rights, property, and freedom from assault in the classroom or playground is addressed through school discipline. In adulthood, the same behaviors against others become violations of the law and prosecuted by courts of law with fines and incarceration among the consequences. Teachers have a duty not just to their students, but also to society to effectively guide and discipline children to reduce or eliminate problem behaviors.

BULLIES WITH GIFTED ABILITIES

Some gifted children have characteristics of intensity, sensitivity, and overexcitability. Overexcitabilities are inborn, heightened abilities to receive and respond to stimuli and appear as increased sensitivity, awareness, and intensity to many things, persons, and events. Emotional and physical manifestations in children include stomachaches, blushing, concern with death, or depression. Such children have a great capacity for deep relationships and show strong emotional attachments to people, places, and things. They have compassion, empathy, and sensitivity in relationships, which can lead to interpersonal conflict with others about the depth, or lack of depth, in a relationship. Children high in emotional overexcitability are often accused of overreacting. Children need teachers to recognize and validate these feelings rather than belittle or ignore them. Teachers can help set boundaries and guide children how to express themselves. Children's compassion and concern for others, their focus on relationships, and the intensity of their feelings may interfere with insignificant everyday tasks compared with the needs of humanity (Lind, 2000). A simple task or a simple question about something that most people find relatively straightforward may draw a response worthy of a doctoral dissertation. Teachers can direct gifted children toward finding appropriate practical responses for the classroom within their more expansive and in-depth contemplations. "Give us a simple answer first" or, "What are the one or two core issues among all the issues?"

Stephanie S. Tolan (1990), author of children's books, puts it succinctly, "The difficulty with highly gifted children in school may be summarized in three words: they don't fit." They may seem uncooperative. Rita Dickinson (1970) found half the children she tested with IQ scores of 132 or above were referred for behavior problems and not seen as gifted by their teachers or parents. Ellen Winner (1997) described Jonathan Estrada, who began talking at nine months, reading at the second grade level at two-and-a-half years, and speaking at that age with an eight-year-old vocabulary. He refused to do "easy" things with blocks the school district's gifted-and-talented program evaluator wanted him to do and was not accepted into the program. Academic misfit is a consistent problem. There may be dyssynchrony—a lack of a natural fit between gifted children and curriculum designed to be developmentally appropriate for children of similar ages with the typical spectrum of abilities. The No Child Left Behind Act (NCLB), which mandates bringing every student to minimum levels of proficiency, may have unfortunate consequences for gifted children. Susan Goldkin, executive director of the California Learning Strategies Center, and David Gold, lecturer and consultant on strategic issues in negotiation, state

> No Child is particularly destructive to bright young math students. Faced with a mandate to bring every last student to proficiency, schools emphasize incessant drilling of rudimentary facts and teach that there is one "right" way to solve even higher-order problems. Yet one of the clearest markers of a nimble math mind is the ability to see novel approaches and shortcuts to attacking such problems. This creativity is what makes math interesting and fun

for those students. Schools should encourage this higher-order thinking, but high-ability students are instead admonished for solving problems the wrong way, despite getting the right answers. Frustrated, and bored by simplistic drills, many come to hate math. (Goldkin & Gold, 2007, ¶ 4)

They feel that the progression of gifted children in language arts also suffers as instruction emphasizes grade-level proficiency versus enrichment at children's levels of competency. An educational approach geared to minimal skills proficiency for lower performing students may be inappropriate and may destroy interest in learning for high-ability students.

Gifted children, especially those exceptionally or profoundly gifted, often prefer, like most children, to associate with peers of comparable interests and capacities. Although some educators believe that differentiated instruction in a heterogeneous mainstream classroom can be effective, placement by chronological age may not offer gifted children many (if any) intellectual peers. However, placing gifted children with older children may not match the breadth or depth of understanding or passion for common interests. Some professionals feel that, especially for exceptionally and profoundly gifted, the only socially compatible peer group may be with other children with comparably gifted abilities (Lovecky, 1995). The study by Gross (1994) of forty Australian gifted children found that gifted children who were retained at their chronological age grade level (or promoted one year) underachieved an average of five years from their tested math and reading abilities. Self-esteem ratings scored more than one standard deviation below other children. In contrast, gifted children who were gradually accelerated a total of three or more years did not underachieve. They also had comparable positive self ratings relative to their older classmates. An article (Bauer, 2007) about online high schools says,

Kevin Johnson remembers the fourth grade painfully well. It was the year educators finally diagnosed the communication chasm that separated him from other children: He is a genius. "That was the worse year emotionally," recalls his mom, Holly. "He didn't mix well with the other students. Kids picked on him because he had a different vocabulary and spoke differently." (p. B1)

The article ends with

for Kevin, there is no turning back. He said he has made friends through his school's field trips and interactive classes. He contacts them outside of school and takes time to socialize. He likes talking the same language as his classmates, he said. . . ."We all speak the same gibberish," Kevin said. (p. B1)

Gibberish to others may be the peer language and culture of children who are exceptionally and profoundly gifted. Getting along and fitting in promotes happiness and self-esteem in gifted children as it does for all children.

Gifted children may experience frustration, depression, and anxiety also suffered by other children with challenges. However, they may experience it all much more intensely. For some gifted children, bullying others to gain self-esteem and power can become a way to compensate. Emotionally aroused, overexcited bullies may bully crudely. This may make them more readily identifiable, while other more restrained and calculating children may escape notice. Peterson and Ray (2006) found that while 67% of 432 gifted eighth-grade participants experienced being bullied in their school careers, 28% of participants also admitted bullying other children. The percentage of bullies increased fairly steadily throughout the school years, from 3% in kindergarten to 16% in eighth grade (p. 157). Gifted children, because of their skills, creativity, or charm, may be well liked by teachers. McGrath (2006) debunks the myth that only outcasts will bully others. Confident bullies, often popular for their powerful personalities, may feel entitled to manipulate and ostracize inferiors while charming others, especially teachers. Some of the most malicious and covert bullies are students popular with teachers. They bully, but play innocent when their victims tell on them. Teachers may respond with disbelief, inaction, or even retaliatory action toward the victim-complainant. If teachers do not hold bullies who are gifted to the same standards of conduct as other children, it confirms their sense of superiority and entitlement to bully and manipulate "inferior" classmates. Despite being derived from different reasons, the sense of superiority is similar to bullies with AS. Boundaries and rules are not for them. They are for the other kids—the "inferior" ones. Teachers need to be aware of their potential prejudice favoring charming children in general or gifted children in particular. Children depend on teachers not to automatically dismiss their complaints against any fellow student. Being consistent with discipline is critical to counter any entitlement to bullying.

Teachers and parents tend to be more alert to physical forms of aggression and bullying. They may minimize verbal teasing, taunting, or bullying as "just kidding." "Sticks and stones may break my bones, but words will never hurt me . . . *not!*" Some gifted children flaunt intellectual and verbal superiority to bully classmates of average ability. This may be a defense against feelings of inadequacy from being misfits. Children with high verbal skills often experience and interpret situations differently and feel compelled to adamantly share their resultant solutions. Knowing they are correct, some gifted children feel entitled to persist asserting themselves. This may not be well received by classmates. The National Association for Gifted Children (2008) Web site, under Peer Relationships/Social Skills/Bullies, has pointers on "How Not to Make Friends." The pointers reflect issues of verbal assertiveness as they caution gifted children to refrain from

- being bossy,
- telling others how to play,
- telling others they are doing things wrong,
- being too intense or serious,
- talking about themselves a lot,
- being negative, using ridicule or sarcasm, and
- bragging.

Gifted children may not understand why others don't accept their recommendations—"But I'm right!"—or why others are annoyed or angry when they insist on telling them again, "But I'm right!" Other children may interpret the verbal assertiveness as intimidating or dominating. Verbal assertiveness can evolve into verbal bullying, as they try to force others to acknowledge that they are correct. "Can't you see? You must be stupid!"

> Many gifted children who exhibit this behavior may be reflecting a sense of intellectual superiority instilled in them by their parents. These children may be victims of being reinforced only for their brainpower at the expense of their humanity. When parents focus all of their energy on the intellect of the child, they are developing a very narrow person. Frequently, the freewheeling fun of childhood is exchanged for a highly structured daily schedule that develops the child into an information bank with deficient social skills. (*Socially inappropriate behaviors*, n.d., p. 1)

The smartest children in the classroom will not be happy children unless they are also socially adept. Simply put, they need friends. Without friends, even children with the greatest of abilities will slide into loneliness and eventual despair. When individuals despair, they often revert to original training or to embedded processes to regain stability or self-worth. Sometimes, when individuals feel desperate, the embedded training from the family models is to assert superiority or to intimidate others. However, as guerrilla warriors follow no accepted rules of warfare, desperate individuals feeling under social assault may ignore social propriety. Guerrilla warriors experience the enemy as mercilessly omnipotent and feel entitled to seek vengeance by any means available. Verbal fluency, cognitive agility, and psychological insight become the weapons of choice and necessity of some children against their tormentors and perceived inferiors. These strengths need to be directed toward problem solving, negotiation, compromise, and developing consensus. Rather than used to "win" or to "defeat" others, these strengths need to be directed to develop understanding, compassion, and empathy. Core feelings and needs are then recognized as universal human issues whatever one's abilities. Empathy counters the superiority versus inferiority philosophy underlying the verbal psychological warfare. "Revenge of the nerds" cyberbullying, as described on the stopcyberbullying.org Web site, unfortunately, may be an almost perfect technique for children who engage in psychological warfare. Cyberspace has relatively fewer boundaries and consequences versus being in school. Verbal fluency, cognitive agility, and psychological insight can flourish without much restraint—to bully.

> Revenge of the Nerds cyberbullies usually target their victims one-on-one and the cyberbully often keeps their activities secret from their friends. If they share their actions, they are doing it only with others they feel would be sympathetic. They rarely appreciate the seriousness of their actions. They also often resort to cyberbullying-by-proxy. Because of this and their tech skills, they can be the most dangerous of all cyberbullies. (*What methods work,* "Power Hungry" and "Revenge of the Nerds" section, ¶ 3)

Boundaries that have historically been maintained with varied success in the physical environment have been further challenged by the free flow and accessibility of modern technology. That technologically savvy children have explored and experimented extensively is not surprising. It is also not surprising that some individuals use their creativity to exploit technology to intensify and broaden the impact of demeaning and insulting communication. The use of technology is not confined to gifted children. It merely offers another means to continue verbal abuse. Peterson and Ray (2006) found that gifted children were increasingly perpetrators of name-calling through Grade 8, from 4% in kindergarten to 14% in Grade 8, while victims with gifted abilities experienced less name calling after Grade 6. Also, gifted bullies began to use more kinds of bullying in Grade 6 (pp. 157–158). This result may be reflective of gifted children being more creative bullies along with cognitive maturity. A disturbing finding was the increase of violent thoughts and deeds as gifted children grew older. Violent thoughts increased from 5% in kindergarten to 16% in fourth grade and 29% in eighth grade, while violent deeds increased 3% in kindergarten to 10% in fourth grade and peaked at 12% in the sixth and seventh grades. Males showed higher percentages than females in both categories, with highs of 37% in thoughts in the eighth grade and 19% in deeds in the sixth grade. These statistics may be hypothesized as a consequence of growing creativity and entitlement along with deepening anger, despair, and alienation. Sometimes teachers fail to recognize that gifted abilities offer no immunity against children becoming bullies. Gifted abilities also do not necessarily offer any advantage for handling difficult emotional and social challenges. Teachers need to be alert for creative aggression from gifted children that would be atypical of other children and aware of the possible heightened intensity of negative feelings for the same children. Intervention should be about activating and directing possible strengths of creativity, emotional intuition, and psychological awareness.

Chapter Highlights

- Asperger syndrome shows a range of symptom severity. This means less impaired children may meet criteria but not get diagnosed. They seem a bit unusual, different, or may be misdiagnosed with ADHD and emotional disturbance.
- Children with Asperger syndrome may be particularly prone to self-righteous vengeance because they often feel victimized for no apparent reason they can discern.
- Adult management enforcing peer acceptance gradually may break down in later grades as teachers' priorities shift from socialization to curriculum demands.
- One reaction to realization of being different is to become arrogant, with intolerant standards and expectations of others.
- Problematic behavior that violates classmates' rights, property, and freedom from assault in the classroom or playground is addressed through school discipline. In adulthood, the same behaviors against others become violations of the law and prosecuted by courts of law with fines and incarceration among the consequences.
- Children with overexcitability may feel every issue more deeply and more intensely.
- Confident bullies, often popular for their powerful personalities, may feel entitled to manipulate and ostracize inferiors while charming others, especially teachers.
- Knowing they are correct, some children with gifted cognitive abilities may feel entitled to persist in asserting themselves. This may not be well received by classmates.
- Verbal fluency, cognitive agility, and psychological insight become the weapons of choice and necessity of some children with gifted abilities against their tormentors and perceived inferiors.

11

Motivation and Survival

ADULT STRESS, FRUSTRATION, FAILURE (AND SUFFERING)

The healthiest and most stable adults can find working with or raising children to be challenging. Some adults may be ill-prepared from their own models and experiences of teaching or caregiving to meet the needs of relatively easygoing children. Encountering more challenging and even incomprehensible behaviors can activate extreme stress or frustration. Some adults may revert to negative patterns of behaviors or experiment with creative but problematic responses to get children to behave. Unfortunately, punishment, followed by more severe punishment, followed by even more severe or "innovative" punishment is often the default response of frustrated adults. Increasingly more severe punishment may be not only an original model of discipline, but also encouraged by various dogmatic "experts." Adults may resort to intimidating, punishing, and forcing young children to toe the line. "You better listen to me! You better . . . or else . . ." The "or else" implied is often a severe consequence, perhaps a severe punishment that would make adults cringe. Children assume and fear that "or else" must be really bad!

Children with challenges are often unable to identify, track, and explain how their particular challenge and their cognitive, emotional, and social circumstances lead to often-frustrating choices and behaviors. Unfortunately, there are some adults who dismiss children's challenges as excuses to misbehave or be lazy. Prejudiced or uniformed teachers label such children as "bad kids." As unemancipated, relatively powerless youth, children often must just endure negative adults' actions. Children who try to assert themselves may be pathologized with diagnoses such as ODD ("bad boys," "bad girls," "disrespectful punks") and suffer major punishments. Teachers should listen to their own voices, the labels they use for children, their tone and their impatience. Having a sense of humor about children and their behavior is important. Humor allows individuals in challenging situations to find perspective. "Now, *that* was really creative! Wow! That's a kindergarten first!" Humor conveys playfulness and facilitates continued affection and connection despite difficulties relating or working together. "Honey, I didn't think you could put something that big into something that small!" Self-deprecating individuals in high-stress situations maintain their sanity better. Teaching is a very serious business, but it is also a serious avocation. It is work, but it is deeply personal. It can be very hard, but very rewarding. Enjoy!

Sadly, some adults enjoy controlling children. Younger children tend to give in to adult domination. They cannot do much about it until they become teenagers. But oh my, then do they do something about it! It can be funny to watch how arrogant assumptions that children can be controlled explode in some adults' faces. Adults, both teachers and parents, find they can no longer get away with it because of changes in adult-teen dynamics and peer relationships. "Or else" is exposed as an empty threat, especially as the need for adult acceptance diminishes and is replaced by growing peer affiliation. Over time, compliance with adults becomes gradually unnecessary for children to survive emotionally, psychologically, and most of all, socially.

"OR ELSE WHAT?"

The threat of "Do it or else!" was effective because of younger children's emotional, social, and functional dependence. Children threatened with physical domination, including corporal punishment, cannot resist or survive without adult support. "Do it or else I'll take it away!" "You won't get any free time!" "You're on time-out!" However as children near adolescence, they realize adults cannot make them eat strained spinach, or ingest values, or pull learning and responsibility out of them.

"You better not ditch school, or else I'll bring you to school every day!"

[Yeah, right. Like there isn't a back gate to the school! Whatcha gonna do? Quit work to watch over me all day in school!?]

"You better sit down! You better . . . or else . . ."

[Or else, what? What are you going to do? I don't have to listen to you. I'm outta here!]

Frustrated and confounded by children's disruptive behaviors, the completion of "or else . . ." implicitly becomes, "I won't love you anymore," or "I'll reject you!" Or it can become the unholy trio of school responses: detention, suspension, and expulsion. After suffering years of negativity, many children with challenges come to hate school and teachers or home and family. Suspension or expulsion from the school they despise loses its threat. Is rejection or exclusion used to motivate children to stop problematic behavior or increase desirable behavior? It is important to find and develop other ways to motivate children besides threats, since threats will eventually lose their impact. As children get older, they gravitate toward approval from peers, expectations of popular culture, and being "cool." In some groups, it is not cool to do well in school. High social status comes from negativity and destructive behavior.

Anton, a youth with ADHD, bragged to me how his defiance and menacing antisocial behavior had developed through elementary school into middle school and high school. His defiant behavior and multiple piercings gained him notoriety among his peers. His behavior frightened and prejudiced school officials and they were often unfairly punitive with him. With barely concealed regret, Anton accepted his compromised academic achievement after experiencing years of learning failures. It was acceptable because status among his peers was now more important. He associated with a crew of other boys, many also with ADHD and similar personas. Adults could no longer intimidate Anton with empty threats because he had given up trying to please adults long ago. Children with LD who cannot keep up academically may congregate in resource classes not for the teacher's academic support but to socialize with other "dummies." The two or three gifted children in the classroom may gravitate to each other, avoiding teachers who don't "get it." Trying to please adults to survive emotionally and socially isn't motivating anymore. In a way, some children accept the "or else." They accept the rejection and seek other validation. The gang of misfits may not have much going for them, but at least they have each other.

INTERNALIZED MOTIVATION

Some preteens and teenagers told me they had lied and deceived adults regularly from early childhood. "I dunno." "I didn't do it." Younger children often opt for convenience, avoidance of hassles, or gaining a perceived benefit in the immediate situation. Without strong adult guidance and discipline, lying can evolve into a habit. As they get older, they feel they are not the people adults wanted them to be.

Teachers and parents work very hard to ensure that children behave more or less appropriately (or feign appropriate behavior) until it all falls apart in adolescence. Strict management and harsh discipline without attention to individual children's needs, personalities, and challenges often backfire, creating resentment and rebellion. Motivating through praise, rewards, or punishment focuses children on praise, rewards, or punishment rather than on internalizing values or even whether the behavior is appropriate or not. Whether or not one gets caught and punished determines if the behavior was appropriate. If not caught and punished (negative motivation), the default consideration of the behavior is that it was OK despite harm to self or others, trust broken, boundaries violated, and values manifested. When children become dependent on others for motivation, no matter how it is positively presented, and then find themselves in a situation where no one is there to provide positive motivation, then . . . nothing happens. Internalized motivation must be the goal of guidance with children. When teachers set boundaries, they also need to help children develop self-definitions based on healthy personal and social values. Feedback should focus children on who and what they may want to be: "Stop, that won't be nice. I don't think you want to be mean." Teacher discipline will be most effective if children's internalized values are activated to guide their choices: "What would be a good choice for you and others now?" Internalized motivation enables individuals to progress in life, resist peer pressure and media messages, and make healthy decisions.

Internalized motivation may be the most critical aspect of gifted children. Determining which areas develop into gifted abilities may depend on the combination of what Lovecky (2004) describes as three aspects of giftedness.

> Giftedness can be defined . . . as *cognition* (precocious development, high cognitive ability, reasoning ability, creative ability), *conation* (high motivation, a passion to master), and *emotion* (intense emotional experiences, sensitivity, compassion and empathy). These aspects of cognition, conation and emotion are not really independent of each other. Creativity, for example, requires ability, a problem to work on, an intense desire to know the answer to the problem, and a passion to overcome obstacles to find out the answer. (p. 38)

Conation may be the most distinguishing aspect between very bright individuals with mediocre performance and noteworthy geniuses. Motivation may separate "gifted, but" individuals from gifted and successful individuals. Comments like, "He's so bright, but . . ." or "She was so outstanding, but . . ." reflect adult regret of lost human potential. "While the ability for cognitive learning is in the brain, the motivation for learning, for inner growth, for self actualization is emotional and is in the heart.

Gifted children are often driven to learn. The drive is emotional; the ability to learn is cognitive" (Roeper, 2004, ¶ 3). In a review of the Cambridge Handbook of Expertise and Expert (Ericsson, Charness, Feltovich, & Hoffman, 2006), David Dobbs (2006) wrote,

> So what does create genius or extreme talent? Musicians have an old joke about this: How do you get to Carnegie Hall from here? Practise. A sober look at any field shows that the top performers are rarely more gifted than the also-rans, but they almost invariably outwork them. This doesn't mean that some people aren't more athletic or smarter than others. The elite are elite partly because they have some genetic gifts—for learning and hand-eye coordination, for instance—but the very best rise because they take great pains to maximise that gift. (Extraordinary Efforts section, ¶ 9)

A natural gift of intense motivation may be the key characteristic or ability as to whether individuals produce gifted performances. Unfortunately, frequent or consistent frustration may dampen and even destroy children's motivations to explore, experiment, and succeed.

Internalized motivation is also related to self-esteem, particularly to what Coopersmith (1967) calls moral virtue. Coopersmith concluded that people base their self-image or self-esteem on four components: significance, moral virtue, power, and competence. Significance is experiencing that you are significant or important to the people significant or important to you. Children's parents, teachers, and eventually peers are significant. Misunderstood children, especially children with challenges, can become disliked and disrespected. They often lack messages of positive significance from others. Moral virtue refers to living up to one's self-definition of being a good (moral and virtuous) person. Self-definition begins with significant adults' perceptions of children projected back to them. How parents see and experience children becomes internalized as children's initial self-definition. Negative feedback causes distress that may trigger behavior inconsistent with children's self-definition of being "good." Being "good" goes beyond behavior and emphasizes children's attitudes, values, and beliefs underlying any choices or behavior. Positive feedback that is internalized creates motivation to behave as the feedback implies. When motivated to live and perform according to what one considers virtuous, other people's presence, approval, or rewards, while gratifying, are not the essential measure of healthy moral living. Self-approval or confirmation becomes the measure of self-worth. Competence, the fourth component, involves having the skills to handle tasks that are important or compelling. Children with challenges are often competent in areas unvalued by others or themselves and incompetent in areas valued by others. This is why teachers and adults need to recognize and validate the uniqueness and strengths of every child, rather than focus only on their challenges.

CULTURAL CHARACTERISTICS
OF CHILDREN WITH CHALLENGES

Children feel compelled to fit in with their classmates. To do so, they often develop a characteristic culture. The following strategies reflect common cultural attitudes, values, and behaviors of children with challenges:

1. Try to be the same as others

2. Hide, avoid, deny, or minimize differences or difficulties (including emotional distress)

3. Work hard or harder than others

4. Quit trying

5. Compensate for differences, difficulties, or challenges

Unsuccessful attempts at the first four strategies can complicate children's lives by causing them to appear even more different from others and may also preclude adult support. Teacher awareness of these strategies is key to guiding children, whether the strategies are relatively effective or highly unsuccessful. Relative effectiveness could mean that children have hidden their needs, are highly stressed from working so hard, or have given up trying. Unsuccessful attempts refer to failure to succeed academically or not fitting in socially. When teachers recognize these strategies, they can then guide children to the final strategy of academically and socially acceptable compensations, which often build upon their strengths.

"That's a Stupid Job!"

Children with LD often avoid reading or writing. They may become motivated to avoid humiliation, because exposing their disabilities to others can be corrosive to their self-esteem. Several of my young clients who had LD that harmed their academic success had parents who also suffered similar problems in childhood. The parents admitted lifelong avoidance of responsibilities or jobs involving reading or writing reports. The avoidance began in elementary school, and eventually resulted in loss of innumerable opportunities for career advancement in adulthood. The parents were adamant that their own children not repeat their avoidance of short-term "hard" things to their long-term detriment. However, they did not know how to support their children. Their own struggles in childhood had not been identified sufficiently for them to have successfully developed interventions. They had not been taught appropriate compensations. Most of their lives, they hid their shame and their LD, often with angry dismissals that diverted others from the hidden core issues. Their children now often duplicated their parents' childhood behaviors.

Although he wanted a part-time job like many other young teens, Martin, a fifteen-year-old derisively rejected fast food jobs, claiming them beneath him. Explanations about how entry-level job experiences lead to better jobs were dismissed. Teachers, vocational workers, and therapists were bewildered and frustrated. Eventually, Martin admitted that he could not make change for money, a requirement for most fast food cashier positions. He had a form of dyscalculia, a learning disability in comprehending mathematics. He was humiliated that what others readily could do was extremely hard for him. In elementary school he would act out, throw tantrums, or become distracting when doing math work. Teachers and classmates thought he was just being a jerk. He *was* being a jerk! And it worked to disguise his LD. The hardest thing for Martin and many other children may be to reveal a challenge or disability that makes them seem different from others. Only when adults identified Martin's dyscalculia could they address it with sensitivity. Only by understanding his motivation to avoid humiliation could adults begin to support his other motivations to succeed. When his dyscalculia was identified and addressed, Martin's other strengths came out. He had an otherwise pleasant personality, good communication skills, creativity, and excellent gross and fine motor skills that became easier to activate and maintain consistently through anticipating and directing compensations when he would be challenged by a calculation. Trying harder is a common strategy for children with LD that sometimes can backfire when it means trying harder at what is ineffective. Trying harder can be turned into a great strength, as it was with Martin, when it is merged with trying differently or creatively as the situation demands. His ingenuity at distracting others from his inability to do math computations "worked." However, when he learned how to compensate for his dyscalculia, his willingness to try harder became effective.

"It's Hard to Be Me"

A child with ADHD said, "It's hard to be me." Compensating for ADHD or other challenging issues may be relatively simple for some and extremely difficult for others. Many children with ADHD manage to do well at school. However, they may come home exhausted from the effort they expend in order to maintain reasonably appropriate behavior. Many parents prioritize school functioning over household functioning. They accept the very distracted, hyperactive, and impulsive, if not chaotic behavior at home as a necessary consequence of greater relative success at school. Doing "better" for children with challenges may consist primarily of resisting their internal energy by being hypervigilant and expending additional nonspontaneous energy—in other words, trying harder. However, children need to have sufficient desire to deal with difficult challenges, whether that means trying harder or attempting other compensations. Without sufficient motivation, children will tend toward simple and easy short-term survival behaviors. Successful compensation depends on children having compelling long-term goals. Children need to be motivated to forgo short-term benefits to reach for and achieve long-term emotional, academic, social, and career opportunities. Dreams must be motivating enough for it to be worth the struggle to face challenges. Otherwise quitting becomes far more attractive than trying harder and differently. The challenge for children with special needs becomes finding dreams that are worth investing hope and energy.

Adults often present college to young children as the optimal opportunity for success and happiness. A college education is meant to be their wonderful dream or the means to other dreams. The United States Census (2006) states approximately 27% of Americans age twenty-five years or older have a bachelor's degree. This means almost three-quarters of Americans age twenty-five or older do not acquire a bachelor's degree. For many children with challenges, elementary through high school is a miserable experience that grinds down their self-esteem. Scolded for being distracted, fidgeting, acting out, and labeled incorrigible, school is anything but fulfilling. Signing on for two to four more years of misery in a community college or a university is not just too hard, but ridiculous! Children may choose to quit trying in school, often years before officially dropping out. Or they may opt out of additional academic or vocational training. Adults should consider whether such children are actually abandoning options for future success.

Certain individuals have aptitudes that make success extremely difficult, yet are successful because they work harder than their less-challenged classmates. Unfortunately, trying harder is not always sufficient. For children with ADHD or other challenges, the hard thing may be to find a fit for their energy and strengths. It is much more likely for a child to feel it is "easy to be me" when adults value the complexity, strengths, challenges, and completeness of the whole "me." Motivating academic and vocational situations for children with ADHD could be where high physical energy, motor-kinesthetic abilities, frequent changes, and short-term focus (versus extended attention) are assets rather than detriments. A child with ADHD probably would not become a researcher of ancient philosophy who must pore intently for hours over ancient text. The focus and limited physical exertion may be too stifling. However, the same child might become a highly energetic daring researcher climbing to the tops of trees deep in the Amazon rainforest. Children are most likely to seize and succeed at opportunities that draw out and exploit their strengths. They are also most likely to struggle and fail at those that accentuate their challenges. Teachers can best present potential gains from facing challenges when balancing them with support and compassion for children's fear of feeling inadequate or stupid . . . again.

"Machines Are Easier"

John Elder Robison (2007) expressed a common preference of some individuals with AS in describing his lifelong affinity with machines and equipment. He says that machines are easier to relate to than people. A LiveScience article on MSNBC.com described digital technology using computerized human figures to successfully teach autistic children advanced social skills. The article asserts it is easier for autistic children to interpret and learn from the computerized images than from actual children (Lloyd, 2008). The virtual human has a more limited presentation of verbal and nonverbal communications, making it easier for the child with autism to interpret, versus interpreting more complex communications from real people. Many individuals with AS gravitate to careers that utilize their affinity with technological and intellectual pursuits, while simultaneously circumscribing social options. Robison always found social interactions and relationships highly challenging. Subsequently, motivated to avoid frustration from interpersonal failures, he gravitated to experiences that minimized social skills. He was unaware he had AS until he was well into adulthood. Later in life, through the support of understanding people, he developed greater social skills. He was able to establish more fulfilling personal and professional relationships. He learned to attend to and correctly interpret facial cues and body language to which he had been previously oblivious. It remains challenging for Robison to interact socially, but he is more purposeful and directed facing his challenges.

Chinese calligraphy often has two words written together with the interplay between the characters creating meaning. The calligraphy for "learning" is composed of "study" on the top and "practice" on the bottom.

Practice doesn't always make perfect, but makes for lots of mistakes! However, practice also develops greater proficiency, and it is critical for learning. Children cannot learn how to be socially proficient by avoiding demanding social situations. Adults need to make it "hard" for children, especially children with challenges. They must provide frequent and consistent social interactions with other children. Study, including study of one's mistakes and considering alternatives, works to facilitate learning. Study for children with AS would involve giving and receiving social cues. They need to process personal choices and experiences for insight and guidance. Study and practice create learning, and learning leads to success. Study and practice are critical to successful compensation for children's challenges. Success makes practice not so hard and success makes "hard" worth it.

Special (Perfection) Is a Hard Fit

Gifted children often have contradictory experiences. All areas of functioning (intellectual, emotional, social, creative, and moral) develop differently, and children with giftedness are not necessarily gifted in all areas. Precocious talents or abilities creating significant strengths, including cognitive awareness, may challenge their emotional maturity. Religious divisiveness, global warming, poverty, genocide, and starvation are intensely complex adult issues. Sunshine or rain today, allowances, mean kids, and snack time and extra snacks are kid issues. These issues can already strain children's emotions and psychology. The motivation to survive for some gifted children may mean hiding their gifts and appearing the same as everyone else. They may try to be not too smart, not too skilled, not too anything in order to fit in. Society promotes all children being special while simultaneously maintaining that everyone is the same. Classrooms may both honor and punish uniqueness. Differences may be honored during classroom celebrations, but classmates become jealous and distrust actual differences in other children. Teachers should not expect gifted children to be preternaturally mature regarding emotional and social situations. Everyone, including the children themselves, needs to recognize that children are children. Children with strong mathematical abilities may handle calculus early. Children with gifted musical abilities may write jazz compositions derivative of Charlie Parker. Children with gifted analytical skills may be able to explain Descartes. However, emotional, psychological, and social sophistication depends deeply on experience. Chronologically young children with limited life experiences cannot, no matter how otherwise gifted, have the wisdom of the ages!

Adults trying to be supportive may unknowingly contribute to the social exclusion of gifted children. They may praise them as exemplary examples to emulate when admonishing their classmates or siblings. "Teacher's pet" remains an insult in today's classroom. It is hard to fit in when the teacher says you're special! Gifted children often see and understand things classmates don't, and feel depths of intensity to which others are oblivious. The hardest thing for gifted children may be trying to relate to classmates, or wanting to be accepted for who they are, but not accepting themselves. Lonely or confused? Sometimes, gifted children think being gifted means they should be beyond the "normal" emotional and psychological turmoil of other children. As supposedly "superhumans," they may feel they should be immune to human emotional turmoil. Yet they cannot help but be human and feel emotions. Gifted children may conclude that they are weirdly blessed and cursed, or that others are stupid or beneath contempt. Self-hatred or superiority may become the two dysfunctional solutions to intrapsychic struggles. It can be hard to find healthy ways to reconcile their gifts among diverse abilities in the larger community. Adults support or retard this process with their relative sophistication about giftedness, the particular gifted abilities, needs, motivations, and so forth of each individual. Adults cannot validate what they do not recognize or understand about gifted children or any children.

Teaching or parenting is craft and science, but it is also art. Guiding children eventually becomes an on-the-spot, in-the-moment decision. Teachers cannot plan for every eventuality. Situations that demand an instantaneous decision without teachers having a full comprehension of all factors will arise. Despite study and exploration about LD, ADHD, AS, giftedness, and more, mistakes with children are inevitable. Stress, frustration, failure, and even suffering will result for both caring adults and children. Single mistakes don't destroy children, but patterns of unrecognized and unaddressed mistakes over time can cause enduring damage. When teachers feel self-doubt and shame, it takes their focus away from children's personalities, development, and needs. Personal demands to be perfect send out a powerful message that perfection is possible and that children must be perfect too. For children with challenges who already feel flawed, perfection is beyond daunting. If adults display disappointment and anger with themselves, they present their fundamental unhappiness and low self-esteem to children, and children emulate their adults, primarily parents and teachers. Models of adult self-love, honesty, and humanity—of compassion for oneself—are the best messages for developing children's self-esteem and health.

Chapter Highlights

- Adults may revert to negative patterns of behaviors or experiment with creative but problematic responses to get children to behave.

- Over time, compliance with adults becomes gradually unnecessary for children to survive emotionally, psychologically, and most of all, socially.

- Internalized motivation enables individuals to progress in life, resist peer pressure and media messages, and make healthy decisions.

- When motivated to live and perform according to what one considers virtuous, other people's presence, approval, or rewards, while gratifying, are not the essential measure of healthy moral living.

- Children with learning disabilities may become motivated to avoid humiliation, because exposing their disabilities to others can be so corrosive to their self-esteem.

- Dreams must be motivating enough for it to be worth the struggle to face challenges. Otherwise quitting becomes far more attractive to some children than trying harder and differently.

- Children cannot learn how to be socially proficient by avoiding demanding social situations.

- Sometimes, others and children with gifted abilities themselves think being gifted means they should be beyond the "normal" emotional and psychological turmoil of "normal" children.

Conclusion

THE NINETY-SECOND-A-DAY
SELF-ESTEEM PRESCRIPTION PLAN

A Truffle a Week

I often supervised therapists using the coffee shop across from our agency. Agency rooms were reserved for client sessions and the shop had areas suitable for confidential meetings. Before starting, we'd get tea or coffee to drink and sometimes a snack. By the cash register were decadent chocolate truffles. An ingredient in chocolate is very similar to THC, the active ingredient in marijuana. Chocolate activates a hormone in the brain similarly activated when in love. Hmmm? No wonder there are so many chocoholics! I would purchase a truffle . . . $1.50, not a big deal. Later, I would give it to my chocolate-loving wife. Big deal? *Big deal!* What did a dose of cocoa and sugar laced with liqueur, not to mention massive calories, mean to my wife? It meant that I think of my wife when not with her. That I know her . . . her preference for dark chocolate, not milk chocolate, and *never* white chocolate! Have I been paying attention for the last thirty-six years? I'd better! And I enjoy delighting her with this simple token. This message conveys confirmation of her value to me. What happens to relationships when such messages are conveyed regularly or if validating messages are irregularly or rarely given?

A Mere Five Seconds . . .

Adults may feel too overwhelmed to devote special time to build children's self-esteem. Not an acceptable excuse with the "Ninety-Second-a-Day Self-Esteem Prescription Plan"! In ninety seconds a day, adults can build children's self-esteem! Numerous opportunities to build self-esteem occur in the daily interactions between adults and children. For example, here's a list of common communications or situations in the household between adults and children. Each one of these offers an opportunity to build children's self-esteem.

1. "I'm tired." (Child yawns)
2. "Where's my brush?"
3. "Where's my shirt?"
4. "I can't find the matching sock!"
5. "Please tie my shoes."
6. "Where's my backpack?"
7. "Can I have pancakes today?"
8. "What are you reading?"
9. "Is it going to rain tomorrow?"
10. "I'm hungry! What can I eat?"
11. "Can I go to Kathy's house tomorrow after school?"
12. "Can I have some more spaghetti?"
13. "Can I watch the baseball game?"
14. "Whatcha doin'?"
15. "This game is cool!"
16. "Who was that?"
17. "Good night."
18. "Are you taking me to school tomorrow?"

Add to each one of these interactions that may occur daily between adults and children. Assuming eighteen such interactions daily, add a mere five seconds to each interaction: *18 opportunities × 5 seconds = 90 seconds.* Not even the whole ninety seconds at a time! Instead of just giving a functional response to give information or answer a question or request, add a simple five-second "message of worth" to each interaction.

- "Time to get up. *I know it's hard, but it's time to get up.*"
- "Over there by the dryer . . . *there's your favorite Spider-Man shirt.*"
- "There's fruit . . . *those purple grapes you really like.*"
- "Good night. *Sweet dreams, honey. Love you.*"

What are the "messages of worth" that adults can add to the normal informative responses? Each of the simple additional communications conveys interest and care in the child. They

- acknowledge that it is difficult for the child to wake up,
- show you are attentive enough to know your child has a favorite Spider-Man shirt,
- nourish the child with food while nurturing him or her with favorite and healthy treats,
- express caring to send the child to the night's rest with a message of love.

Children's self-esteem grows and solidifies when they know what they feel and experience matters. Every interaction potentially conveys communication about children's worth. Beyond words, tone, body language, facial expressions, actions, and lack of actions are messages of worth or unworthiness. Frustrated or distracted teachers and parents may react to children with challenges without regard to how their implicit communications impact the children's self-esteem. Adults may address the function of the communication request without validating the worth of individuals making the request. Communication between two intimates is often more than merely an information exchange, as demonstrated when comparing the adult-child pair to an adult couple. Gottman, Murray, Swanson, Tyson, and Swanson (2002), in their theory of marital relations, note that

> couples make what we now call "bids" for emotional connection. These bids can be as simple as bids for attention (e.g., "Isn't that a pretty boat?"), or they can be requests for emotional support (e.g., "I am worried about my sister"). Unhappily married couples make far fewer bids than happily married couples and the probability of a partner turning away from a bid for connection is much higher among the unhappily married. In all marriages, the probability of rebidding once a partner turns away is nearly zero. . . . it is important to make an emotional connection . . . It need not be an empathetic response or validation. It can be genuine interest. The intervention is simply to make these moments mindful instead of mindless moments (in which people are on automatic pilot and not noticing their partners' bids for connection). (pp. 308–309)

Children's bids to adults and peers are essentially the same as those between couples. Unbidden communication initiated by adults can offer attention and emotional connections. However, adult responses to children's bids may be more important to meet children's needs for validation and nurturing. Children need "genuine interest" from their adults. Poorly nurtured children in unhappy and unfulfilling relationships may be modeling their future relationships. Consistently adding five-second messages of worth to otherwise mindless interactions builds children's self-esteem in ninety seconds a day! Imagine if at work, school, or otherwise, the communication autopilots could be changed so that every interaction or communication received from others included a five-second message of worth! The world would be such a better place! Is this a "trick" solution? Of course, it's a "trick" but not because it doesn't work. It is a "trick" because following through on the solution requires supreme focus. Only emotionally healthy adults can follow through on the Ninety-Second-a-Day Prescription Plan. If life is overwhelming, if stress is debilitating, or if focus is constantly drawn to crises, it becomes difficult to consistently add messages of worth to communications. Tragically, some individuals consistently give messages of unworthiness that destroy others' self-esteem. Teachers see how toxic energy invades their interactions with children. Personal mental health will always be a foundation for effective teaching.

A Community of Messages

The earlier examples were primarily from parent-child interactions. Interactions and messages of worth are often the same in classrooms. However, teachers may not have eighteen distinct daily interactions with each student in their classrooms. Some interactions and messages of worth may be from teachers to the entire classroom or to small groups of children. Multiple classroom tasks and demands can already feel overwhelming, but teachers should not to be tempted to forgo the individual relationships that are at the core of teaching and learning.

> Relationships with children, regardless of age, develop one at a time, over time. Each relationship is precious. Teachers build relationships with children by recognizing, respecting, gaining knowledge about, and making a commitment to each child. A good teacher-child relationship may be even more valuable for children with behavior and learning challenges . . . so teachers need to learn which children need more of their attention and time. The very good news is that the investment of attention and time in service of building a relationship is never wasted. When teachers support children's learning to recognize, respect, know, and commit to others, they are supporting development of the most essential social skills—those that develop and maintain relationships. (Gallagher & Mayer, 2006, pp. 46–47)

Human services can be defined as offering oneself in a relationship with another person. Depending on the professional roles, relationships include reparative, supportive, mentoring, and especially learning relationships. The intimate relationship between a teacher and a student may be second only to that of a parent and a child in its formative power. A highly skilled and exceptional teacher can create the illusion for every child of being the teacher's favorite. Children with highly challenging behaviors or learning issues do better when they feel teachers like them. And children know if teachers or a particular adult likes them. A mother told me how her daughter Aria would have a good year where she enjoyed school despite having some behavior problems. She would show improvements over the year. That would be followed by a bad year where she hated school and had horrific behavior problems. In the bad year, she regressed. Then there would be another good year or perhaps, a bad year. Initially, it was not clear why Aria had such qualitatively different experiences from school year to school year. While I was working with them, Aria was having a very bad school year, exhibiting a number of negative behaviors: throwing tantrums, arguing, getting into fights, and more. Her mother was talking about this mystery with Aria's teacher, Ms. Yee, from the previous year. Ms. Yee responded, "She had all those problems last year too." Although Aria had the same behavior problems last year, she had a good year. She had loved school. Why? It turned out that she loved her teacher last year. More important, Ms. Yee liked Aria and cared about her. She accepted that her responsibility included dealing with Aria's emotional and behavioral problems. This year her teacher, Ms. Gordon, resented that Aria was not ready to learn because of her challenging issues. As Ms. Gordon punished Aria with resentment, intolerance, and negativity, Aria punished her back by retaliating with her full arsenal of negative behaviors. Ms. Yee tried to teach Aria. Ms. Gordon taught third grade. She taught class, she taught lessons, but she didn't teach Aria. Teaching at its best is still a one-to-one relationship.

Teachers should remember that they cannot and do not provide all the relationships in a classroom. The healthiest classrooms activate children as classroom citizens that provide enriching relationships, serving each other in many ways. Children become quickly aware of classmates' individuality. They may not know Dwight has dyslexia, but know he struggles with reading. Many of them like helping Dwight with reading. Catie describes any group over four items as "a lot." "One, two, three, four . . . a lot!" That's kind of cute. Five is a lot of cookies! They don't know the difference between ADHD and their ABCs, but they notice Izumi likes to touch everything, especially anything new. He has great ideas for playing. He's so fun sometimes! Asparagus is a vegetable some may like, but Asperger syndrome is meaningless to them. However, they worry when Nellie gets agitated over the itchiness of his shirt collar. They know Qani loves singing, but sings songs they've never heard before. Children notice just about everything there is to notice about each other, but often do not pass judgment until and unless others, especially adults, label it as "good" or "bad."

Unless teachers welcome a diversity of children, model attitudes, values, beliefs, and especially behaviors of an inclusive culture, children become intolerant of differences. Inclusion is a reality. Many children considered not disadvantaged enough for special services are now spending their entire school careers in general education classrooms. Dwight, Catie, Izumi, Nellie, and Qani may not have been in mainstream classrooms a generation ago, but they are now. Teachers might not be able to give eighteen individual daily messages of worth to each child, but they can consistently model and promote respect of individuality. Following the teachers' model, children cumulatively can easily surpass eighteen messages of worth to one another. Teachers can institute specific programs such as "Secret Friends," when students do something nice secretly for their secret friends. Or they can have regular times for honoring, when children acknowledge to the class something nice a classmate has done. Or a teacher can promote children helping one another by awarding individual and class helper points redeemable with something special. Eighteen messages of worth for each child? How about five hundred messages of worth every day in every way in the classroom? Teachers can make respect and appreciation integral parts of the culture, leading to wonderful classrooms and delightful children. Children from such classrooms are much more likely to play it forward into an inclusive and progressive society that celebrates diversity.

Good Teachers Already Know

Let's repeat the premise of this book. The more teachers become aware of the wisdom they have acquired working in the general education classroom with typical children, the more they can apply it to working with and supporting children with challenges. Conversely, the more teachers become aware of the wisdom they have acquired working with children with specific challenges, the more they can apply it to working with and supporting all children. Good teachers already know sound principles and techniques generally work. This is especially true when they are tailored to individual needs and strengths. With significant tendencies or particular characteristics, labels such as LD, ADHD, AS, and giftedness may be applied to children. Good teachers already know children are not labels or percentiles but individuals. Good teachers already assess for learning diversity, for social skills, and for complicating issues. Good teachers already diagnose and individualize teaching. They mitigate challenges and accentuate and activate strengths. They face the challenge of inclusion by activating knowledge already possessed. When good teachers incorporate knowledge, experience, and dedication with love of teaching, they become the great teachers that children need.

A LAST THOUGHT

Teaching isn't just about learning this or that. The time, energy, and demands will tire you. It's hard, but because it's hard, it's the right thing to do. If you are doing it correctly, you will be energized. How do you build a powerful teacher? Stress 'em, frustrate 'em, make sure they fail and suffer too! And, with sensitivity and support from colleagues, parents, and others, you will develop skills and strengths. If you can survive, and then flourish, then it'll all be worth it. If you're not having fun, if you're not finding children, especially unique children to be stimulating, delightful and joyful and energetic, then you're doing something wrong. Find the joy of teaching and you will know you are doing it correctly and well.

Chapter Highlights

- Numerous opportunities abound to build self-esteem and occur in the daily interactions between adults and children.

- Beyond words, tone, body language and facial expressions, and actions and lack of actions are messages of worth or unworthiness.

- If life is overwhelming, stress debilitating, or if focus is constantly drawn to crises, it becomes difficult to consistently add messages of worth to communications.

- Children with highly challenging behaviors or learning issues do better when they feel teachers, despite their exasperation and disciplinary responses, still like them.

- The healthiest classrooms activate children as classroom citizens that provide enriching relationships, serving each other in many ways.

- Healthy classrooms involve children to provide each other with frequent messages of worth.

- Find the joy of teaching.

References

American Psychiatric Association. (1994). *Diagnostic and statistical manual of mental disorders* (4th ed.). Washington, DC: Author.

Arnold, E. M., Goldston, D. B., Walsh, A. K., Reboussin, B. A., Daniel, S. S., Hickman, E., & Wood, F. B. (2005). Severity of emotional and behavioral problems among poor and typical readers. *Journal of Abnormal Child Psychology, 33*(2), 205.

Attwood, T. (2006). *The complete guide to Asperger's syndrome.* London and Philadelphia: Jessica Kingsley.

Avildsen, J. (Director). (1984). *The karate kid* [Motion picture]. United States: Columbia Pictures.

Barkley, R. A. (2006). *Attention-deficit hyperactivity disorder: A handbook for diagnosis and treatment* (3rd ed.). New York: Guilford Press.

Bauer, M. (2007, July 30). Online high schools are niche some kids need. *St. Paul Pioneer Press,* p. B1.

Bauer, S. (1996). *Asperger syndrome.* Retrieved February 15, 2008, from http://www.udel.edu/bkirby/asperger/as_thru_years.html

Bazelon, E. (2007, August 5). What autistic girls are made of. *New York Times.* Retrieved August 5, 2007, from http://www.nytimes.com/2007/08/05/magazine/05autism-t.html

Best, K. (2007, August 14). Prioritize the eyes, get checked. *Florida Today.* Retrieved August 15, 2007, from www.floridatoday.com

Blachman, D. R., & Hinshaw, S. P. (2002). Patterns of friendship among girls with and without attention-deficit/hyperactivity disorder. *Journal of Abnormal Child Psychology, 30,* 625–640.

Brasic, J. R. (2006, April 10). Pervasive developmental disorder: Asperger syndrome. *eMedicine.* Retrieved March 2, 2008, from http://www.aspennj.org/pdf/information/articles/pervasive-developmental-disorder.pdf

Bullying (and Asperger syndrome). (n.d.). Retrieved March 16, 2008, from http://www.yourlittleprofessor.com/bullying.html

Can people with Asperger's syndrome bully? (2008). Retrieved February 15, 2008, from http://uk.answers.yahoo.com/question/index;_ylt=AtmTCaSc_hAtC3HCB4F2H49JBgx.;_ylv=3?qid=20070613091645AA6cSCI (No longer available online)

Carter, B. B., & Spencer, V. G. (2006). The fear factor: Bullying and students with disabilities. *International Journal of Special Education, 21*(1), 11–23.

Checkley, K. (2003). Teaching gifted children (and all others) to think better. *Classroom Leadership, 7*(3), 7.

Chiauzzi, E. (2007). *Ritalin abuse, addiction and treatment.* Retrieved January 19, 2009, from http://www.addictionsearch.com/treatment_articles/article/ritalin-abuse-addiction-and-treatment_43.html

Connor, M. (1999). *Autism: Current issues 10.* Retrieved May 15, 2008 from http://www.mugsy.org/connor7.htm

Coopersmith, S. (1967). *The antecedents of self-esteem.* San Francisco: William H. Freeman.

Costas, R. (2008, August 17). Interview with Michael and Debbie Phelps. *2008 Beijing Summer Olympic Games* [Television broadcast]. New York: National Broadcasting Company.

De Palma, B. (Director). (1976). *Carrie* [Motion picture]. United States: United Artists.

De Souza Fleith, D. (2001, Spring). Suicide among gifted adolescents: How to prevent it. *NRC/GT Newsletter.* Retrieved March 2, 2008, from http://www.gifted.uconn.edu/nrcgt/newsletter/spring01/sprng012.html

Dickinson, R. M. (1970). *Caring for the gifted.* North Quincy, MA: Christopher Publishing House.

Dionne, G. (2005). Language development and aggressive behavior. In R. E. Tremblay, W. W. Hartup, & J. Archer (Eds.), *Developmental origins of aggression* (pp. 330–352). New York: Guilford Press.

Dobbs, D. (2006, October 16). E=mc2 (and a lot of hard work). *The Age.* Retrieved April 4, 2008, from http://www.theage.com.au/articles/2006/10/13/1160246332748.html?page=fullpage#contentSwap2

Emotional intelligence. (2002). *Duke Gifted Letter, 2*(2). Retrieved February 24, 2008, from http://www.dukegiftedletter.com/articles/vol2no2_feature.html

Ericsson, A. K., Charness, N., Feltovich, P. J., & Hoffman, R. R. (Eds.). (2006). *Cambridge handbook of expertise and expert performance.* New York: Cambridge University Press.

Famous dyslexics. (n.d.). Retrieved May 12, 2009, from http://www.dyslexia.ca/m/content/article.php?content_id=49

Famous people with dyslexia. (n.d.). Retrieved March 2, 2008, from http://www.happydyslexic.com/node/4

Flora, C. (2006, December). The Kiriana conundrum, *Psychology Today, 39*(6), 96–100.

Flynt, S. W., & Morton, R. C. (2004). Bullying and children with disabilities. *Journal of Instructional Psychology,* December 2004. Retrieved February 17, 2008, from http://findarticles.com/p/articles/mi_m0FCG/is_4_31/ai_n8590245

Gaetano, C. (2006, August 31). General ed. teachers face special ed. realities: Districts, colleges adjust to a changing educational landscape. *East Brunswick Sentinel.* Retrieved February 27, 2007, from http://ebs.gmnews.com/news/2006/0831/Schools/043.html

Gagnon, C., Craig, W. M., Tremblay, R., Zhou, R. M., & Vitaro, F. (1995). Kindergarten predictors of boys' stable behavior problems at the end of elementary school. *Journal of Abnormal Psychology, 23,* 751–766. Retrieved June 17, 2009, http://www.springerlink.com/content/104756/?p=800c778b7ec64662a870c68100a5430f&pi=0

Gallagher, K. C., & Mayer, K. (2006). Teacher-child relationships at the forefront of effective practice. *Young Children, 61*(6), 44–49.

Ghandour, R. M., Overpeck, M. D., Huang, Z. J., Kogan, M. D., & Scheidt, P. C. (2004). Headache, stomachache, backache, and morning fatigue among adolescent girls in the United States: Associations with behavioral, sociodemographic, and environmental factors. *Archives of Pediatric & Adolescent Medicine, 158,* 797–803.

Giedd, J. (2003). ADHD and substance abuse. *Medscape Psychiatry & Mental Health, 8*(1). Retrieved March 3, 2008, from http://www.medscape.com/viewarticle/456199_print

GlaxoSmithKline. (2008). *Highlights of prescribing information: Ventolin HFA.* Retrieved March 3, 2008, from http://us.gsk.com/products/assets/us_ventolin_hfa.pdf

Glew, G. M., Fan, M. Y., Katon, W., Rivara, F. P., & Kernic, M. A. (2005). Bullying, psychosocial adjustment, and academic performance in elementary school. *Archives of Pediatric & Adolescent Medicine, 159,* 1026–1031.

Golding, W. (1954). *Lord of the flies.* United Kingdom: Faber and Faber.

Goldkin, S., & Gold, D. (2007, August 7). The gifted children left behind. *Washington Post,* p. A13. Retrieved August 7, 2007, from http://www.washingtonpost.com/wp-dyn/content/article/2007/08/26/AR2007082600909.html

Goleman, D. (1995). *Emotional intelligence.* New York: Bantam Books.

Gordon, N. J., & Fleisher, W. L. (2002). *Effective interviewing and interrogation techniques.* San Diego, CA: Academic Press.

Gottman, J. M., Murray, J. D., Swanson, C., Tyson, R., and Swanson, K. R. (2002). *The mathematics of marriage: Dynamic nonlinear models.* Cambridge, MA: MIT Press.

Grey's Anatomy's Dempsey has dyslexia. (2006, February 28). *Associated Press.* Retrieved March 2, 2008, from http://www.msnbc.msn.com/id/11610814

Gross, M. U. M. (1994). Factors in the social adjustment and social acceptability of extremely gifted children. *Talent Development, 2,* 473–476. Retrieved February 17, 2008, from http://www.davidsongifted.org/db/Articles_id_10028.aspx

Handford, M. (1987). *Where's Waldo.* Cambridge, MA: Candlewick Press.

Harry, B., & Klingner, J. (2007). Discarding the deficit model. *Educational Leadership, 64*(5), 16–21.

Haskins, B. G., & Silva, J. A. (2006). Asperger's disorder and criminal behavior: Forensic-psychiatric considerations. *Journal of the American Academy of Psychiatry and the Law, 34,* 374–384.

Heinrichs, R., & Myles, B. S. (2003). *Perfect targets: Asperger syndrome and bullying.* Shawnee Mission, KS: Autism Asperger Publishing.

Holmberg, K., & Hjern, A. (2007). Bullying and attention-deficit–hyperactivity disorder in 10-year-olds in a Swedish community. *Developmental Medicine & Child Neurology, 50*(2), 134–138.

Hughes, J. (Director). (1985). *The breakfast club* [Motion picture]. United States: Universal Pictures.

Jackson, P. S., & Peterson, J. (2003). Depressive disorder in highly gifted adolescents. *Journal of Secondary Gifted Education, 14*(3), 175–186. Retrieved May 10, 2009, from http://psych.wisc.edu/henriques/papers/Jackson.pdf

Johnson, B. (2002). Behavior problems in children and adolescents with learning disabilities. *Internet Journal of Mental Health, 1*(2). Retrieved February 16, 2008, from http://www.ispub.com/ostia/index.php?xmlFilePath=journals/ijmh/vol1n2/learning.xml

Kaltiala-Heino, R., Rimpelä, M., Marttunen, M., Rimpelä, A., & Rantanen, P. (1999). Bullying, depression, and suicidal ideation in Finnish adolescents: School survey. *British Medical Journal, 319,* 348–351.

Katz, N., & Zemishlany, Z. (2006). Criminal responsibility in Asperger's syndrome. *Israel Journal of Psychiatry and Related Sciences, 43*(3), 166–173.

Kim, Y. S., Koh, Y. J., & Leventhal, B. L. (2004). Prevalence of school bullying in Korean middle school students. *Archives of Pediatric & Adolescent Medicine, 158,* 737–741.

Ladd, P. (2003). *Understanding deaf culture: In search of deafhood.* Clevedon, England: Multilingual Matters.

Lelchuk, I. (2007, March 17). School bullies' new turf—Internet: Taunted Novato girl's plight illustrates painful phenomenon. *San Francisco Chronicle.* Retrieved March 19, 2007, from http://www.sfgate.com/cgi-bin/article.cgi?f=/c/a/2007/03/17/BULLY.TMP

Lind, S. (2000). Overexcitability and the highly gifted child. *The Communicator, 31*(4), 4. Retrieved May 9, 2009 from http://www.davidsongifted.org/db/Articles_id_10102.aspx

Little, L. (2003). Identifying and preventing the risks for victimization of children with Asperger syndrome. In R. W. DuCharme & T. P. Gullotta (Eds.), *Asperger syndrome: A guide for professionals and families* (pp. 134–156). New York: Kluwer Academic/Plenum.

Lloyd, R. (2008, February 21). Virtual teachers outperform real thing: Digital tutors help children and adults develop advanced skills. *LiveScience.* Retrieved February 22, 2008, from http://www.msnbc.msn.com/id/23276977/

Long Beach City College Foundation. (2004). *Communicate! A workbook for interpersonal communication.* Dubuque, IA: Kendal/Hunt.

Lovecky, D. V. (1995). Highly gifted children and peer relationships. *Counseling and Guidance Newsletter, 5*(3), 2, 6–7. Retrieved February 17, 2008, from http://www.davidsongifted.org/db/Articles_id_10129.aspx

Lovecky, D. V. (2004). *Different minds: Gifted children with AD/HD, Asperger syndrome, and other learning deficits.* London and Philadelphia: Jessica Kingsley.

Mah, R. (2006). *Difficult behavior in early childhood: Positive discipline for preK–3 classrooms and beyond.* Thousand Oaks, CA: Corwin.

Mah, R. (2008). *The one-minute temper tantrum solution.* Thousand Oaks, CA: Corwin.

Mandic, T. (1996). Body language in debating. *Debate Newsletter* (The Karl Popper Debate Program of the Open Society Institute and the Network of Soros Foundations), 2(2). Retrieved March 3, 2008, from http://www.osi.hu/debate/body.htm

Marano, H. E. (1995, September/October). Big bad bully. *Psychology Today, 51–82.*

Maryland Institute Research Reports. (n.d.). *Co-morbidity of attention deficit hyperactivity disorder (ADHD) in sexually aggressive children and adolescents.* Retrieved February 16, 2008, from http://personal.boo.net/~dpfago/research_adhd.htm

Mayer, J. D., Caruso, D. R., & Salovey, P. (1999). Emotional intelligence meets traditional standards for an intelligence. *Intelligence, 27*(4), 267–298.

Mayer, J. D., & Salovey, P. (1997). *What is emotional intelligence? Emotional development and emotional intelligence.* New York: Basic Books.

McGrath, M. J. (2006). *School bullying: Tools for avoiding harm.* Thousand Oaks, CA: Corwin.

McNeil, C. B., Capage, L. C., & Bennett, G. M. (2002). Cultural issues in the treatment of young African American children diagnosed with disruptive behavior disorders. *Journal of Pediatric Psychology, 27*(4), 339–350.

MedlinePlus. (2008). *Dextromethorphan.* Retrieved March 3, 2008, from http://www.nlm.nih.gov/medlineplus/druginfo/meds/a682492.html

Morelock, M. J. (1992). Giftedness: The view from within. *Understanding Our Gifted, 4*(3), 1, 11–15. Retrieved February 17, 2008, from http://www.davidsongifted.org/db/Articles_id_10172.aspx

MSN Encarta Dictionary. (2008). *Theory of mind.* Retrieved May 26, 2008 from http://encarta.msn.com/dictionary_/Theory%2520of%2520Mind.html

Nansel, T. R., Craig, W., Overpeck, M. D., Saluja, G., Ruan, J., & the Health Behaviour in School-aged Children Bullying Analyses Working Group. (2004). Cross-national consistency in the relationship between bullying behaviors and psychosocial adjustment, *Archives of Pediatric & Adolescent Medicine, 158,* 730–736.

National Association for Gifted Children. (2008). *Peer relationships/social skills/bullies.* Retrieved August 23, 2008, from http://www.nagc.org/index.aspx?id=1212

National Center on Addiction and Substance Abuse at Columbia University. (2000). *Substance abuse and learning disabilities: Peas in a pod or apples and oranges?* Retrieved August 22, 2008, from http://www.eric.ed.gov/ERICDocs/data/ericdocs2sql/content_storage_01/0000019b/80/17/01/ad.pdf

Norwich, B., & Kelly, N. (2004). Pupils' views on inclusion: Moderate learning difficulties and bullying in mainstream and special schools. *British Educational Research Journal, 30*(1), 43–65.

Parrot, J. (Director). (1930). *Another fine mess* [Motion picture]. United States: Metro-Goldwin-Meyer.

Parsons, L. (2003). *The classroom troubleshooter: Strategies for dealing with marking and paper-work, discipline, evaluation, and learning through language.* Markham, Ontario, Canada: Pembroke.

Peterson, J. S., & Ray, K. E. (2006). Bullying and the gifted: Victims, perpetrators, prevalence, and effects. *Gifted Child Quarterly, 50,* 148–168.

Pupils "should penalise bullies." (2007, March 28). *BBC News.* Retrieved March 28, 2007, from http://news.bbc.co.uk/1/hi/education/6496725.stm

Risk, protection, and resilience. (2001, September 28). *Research FACTs and Findings.* Retrieved February 26, 2008, from http://www.actforyouth.net/documents/FactSheet1Risk.pdf

Robison, J. E. (2007). *Look me in the eyes.* New York: Crown.

Roeper, A. (2004). The emotional needs of the gifted child. Retrieved February 15, 2008, from http://www.educationoasis.com/resources/Articles/emotional_needs_gifted.htm

Sapolsky, R. (2005, May). *Why zebras don't get ulcers—Stress, disease, and coping.* Paper presented at California Association of Marriage & Family Therapists 2005 Annual Conference, San Jose, CA.

Schwartz-Watts, D. M. (2005). Asperger's disorder and murder. *Journal of the American Academy of Psychiatry and the Law, 33,* 390–393.

Seaward, B. L. (2002). *Managing stress: Principles and strategies for health and well-being* (3rd ed.). Boston: Jones & Bartlett.

Silverman, L. K. (2005). *I'm not gifted, I'm just busy: Unrecognized giftedness in women.* Retrieved June 17, 2009, from www.xi2.nl/bronnen/Resources/I'm%20not%20Gifted .pdf

Simmons, R. (2002). *Odd girl out: The hidden culture of aggression in girls.* New York: Harcourt.

Socially inappropriate behaviors. (n.d.). Retrieved February 15, 2008, from http://www .teachervision.fen.com/behavior-modification/teaching-methods/5841.html

Sonji. (2008). *Children with ADHD—Possible victims or potential bullies.* Retrieved April 25, 2008, from http://hubpages.com/hub/Children-With-ADHD-Possible-Victims-or-Potential-Bullies

Sourander, A., Jensen, P., Rönning, J. A., Elonheimo, H., Niemelä, S., Helenius, H., et al. (2007). Childhood bullies and victims and their risk of criminality in late adolescence: the Finnish from a boy to a man study. *Archives of Pediatric & Adolescent Medicine, 161*(6), 546–552.

Spencer, T., Wilens, T., Biederman, J., Wozniak, J., & Harding-Crawford, M. (2000). Attention-deficit/hyperactivity disorder with mood disorders. In T. Brown (Ed.), *Attention-deficit disorders and comorbidities in children, adolescents, and adults* (pp. 79–123). Washington, DC: American Psychiatric Press.

Stanton, G. H. (1998). *The 8 stages of genocide.* Retrieved August 22, 2008, from http://www.genocidewatch.org/8stages.htm

Tauscher-Wisniewski, S. (2006). Aggression in attention-deficit/hyperactivity disorder children: diagnostic or comorbid symptom? *Expert Review of Neurotherapeutics, 6*(10), 1397–1399.

Thunfors, P., & Cornell, D. (2005). Popularity of middle school bullies. Retrieved May 26, 2008, from http://youthviolence.edschool.virginia.edu/pdf/2006-APA-popularity-of-middle-school-bullies.pdf

Timofeyev, A. V., Sharff, K., Burns, N., & Outterson, R. (2002). *Motivation.* Retrieved March 28, 2008, from http://wso.williams.edu/~atimofey/self_mutilation/Motivation/index.html

Tolan, S. S. (1990). Helping your highly gifted child. *ERIC EC Digest #E477.* (ERIC Document Reproduction Service No. ED321482).

Totten, M., & Quigley, P. (2003). *Bullying, school exclusion and literacy.* Retrieved May 30, 2008, from http://acsp.cpha.ca/antibullying/english/backinfo/CPHA_Discussion_Paper-PDF.pdf

United States Census. (2006). *Percent of people 25 years and over who have completed a bachelor's degree: 2006.* Retrieved March 30, 2008, from http://factfinder.census.gov/servlet/GRTTable?_bm=y&-geo_id=01000US&_box_head_nbr=R1502&-ds_name=ACS_2006_EST_G00_&-format=US-30

Unnever, J. D., & Cornell, D. G. (2003). Bullying, self-control, and ADHD. *Journal of Interpersonal Violence, 18*(2), 129–147.

Vierikko, E., Pulkkinen, L., Kaprio, J., & Rose, R. J. (2004). Genetic and environmental influences on the relationship between aggression and hyperactivity-impulsivity as rated by teachers and parents. *Twin Research, 7*(3), 261–274.

Wallach, L. B. (1994). Violence and young children's development. Urbana, IL: ERIC Clearinghouse on Elementary and Early Childhood Education. (ERIC Document Reproduction Service No. ED369578)

Wargo, E. (2006). The myth of prodigy and why it matters. *Observer, 19*(8). Retrieved March 2, 2008, from http://www.psychologicalscience.org/observer/getArticle.cfm?id=2026

Waters, M. (Director). (2004). *Mean girls* [Motion picture]. United States: Paramount Pictures.

What methods work with the different kinds of cyberbullies? Retrieved May 16, 2008, from http://www.stopcyberbullying.org/parents/howdoyouhandleacyberbully.html

Whitney, R. V. (2002). *Bridging the gap.* New York: Berkley.

Winner, E. (1997). Exceptionally high intelligence and schooling. *American Psychologist, 52*(10), 1070–1081.

Index